STRIVING TOGETHER

STRIVING TOGETHER

A Way Forward in Christian-Muslim Relations

CHARLES KIMBALL

ORBIS BOOKS

Maryknoll, New York 10545

Second Printing, May 1991

The Catholic Foreign Mission Society of America (Maryknoll) recruits and
trains people for overseas missionary service. Through Orbis Books, Maryknoll
aims to foster the international dialogue that is essential to mission. The books
published, however, reflect the opinions of their authors and are not meant to
represent the official position of the society.

Copyright © 1991 by Charles Kimball
Published by Orbis Books, Maryknoll, NY 10545
All rights reserved
Scripture quotations from the New Revised Standard Version of the Bible ©
1990 are used with permission
Manufactured in the United States of America

Library of Congress Cataloging-in-Publication Data

Kimball, Charles.
   Striving together: a way forward in Christian-Muslim relations /
Charles Kimball.
     p. cm.
   Includes bibliographical references.
   ISBN 0-88344-691-X
   1. Islam — Relations — Christianity. 2. Christianity and other
religions — Islam. I. Title.
BP172.K63 1990
261.2'7 — dc20
                                  90-46565
                                      CIP

To Nancy

Contents

Introduction

Interreligious dialogue is a polyphony which, if well orchestrated, can become a rich, symphonic harmony and a dance of all the diversities that compose it. Is it a dream? Maybe. But, it is worth the dream. . . . The Qur'an shows us how a good word can be fertile by this parable: "A good word is as a beautiful tree. Its roots are firm; its branches reach up to the sky; and, in its season, with the help of God, it produces fruit abundantly." Thus, God provides parables to humankind in order that they may think.

—Muhammad Talbi

Far from being impartial or dispassionate, I begin with the conviction that achieving new, more positive relations between Christians and Muslims is a major and urgent item on the world's agenda. Like the Tunisian scholar, Muhammad Talbi, I am persuaded that intentional efforts in interreligious dialogue and the offering of "a good word" can contribute substantially toward a new day in Christian-Muslim relations. A brief overview outlining the nature of my involvement in interfaith issues will help both to make clear my orientation and to set the context for the book.

My paternal grandfather was one of nine children in a Jewish family that emigrated from the Poland/Russia area in the 1880s. Although he married a Presbyterian and their children became Christian, the larger extended family remained Jewish. As a result, I was imbued with a very positive understanding of the Jewish tradition during childhood.

Growing up in Oklahoma, I discovered early on that religious diversity—interreligious or intra-Christian—was not easily affirmed by a substantial portion of those around me. In my community, clear divisions separated Protestants from Roman Catholics. Exclusive claims to truth were common even among Protestants. Many of my friends who were Baptists, for instance, were convinced that the Methodists, Episcopalians, and Presbyterians, among others, were in grave danger of missing the true gospel of Christ. Although there were very few Jews in Tulsa, I recall hearing and reacting strongly to derogatory comments casually uttered about Jews. While most debates between Christians over the differences between communions never struck me as of ultimate consequence, I was troubled deeply by people who made fun of or made disparaging comments about Jews. As a child, I interpreted these as direct ridicule of my grandfather and the extended family. Even at an early age, it was clear that such comments were rooted in an ignorance and prejudice that stood in opposition to my experience and family relationships.

During high school and college, I became deeply involved in my own religious tradition through active participation in a local church and various church-related organizations. In addition, I began an academic study of religion through an undergraduate minor at Oklahoma State. I was both puzzled and intrigued by the relationship between Christian truth claims and the truth claims of others. Three years at The Southern Baptist Theological Seminary in Louisville, Kentucky, provided rich opportunities to pursue the study of world religions and the theological questions related to Christian faith in a religiously plural world. Although the inquiry produced more questions than answers, I discovered it was possible to be a person of faith, a Christian, with integrity and, at the same time, remain open to new discoveries and insights about God's activity in creation. I was fortunate, indeed, to have excellent faculty guidance throughout college and seminary. At each stage, several people nurtured and encouraged this study and theological reflection.

In 1975, I began doctoral study in the History of Religion (Comparative Religion) at Harvard. My area of specialization focussed on Islamic studies and Christian-Muslim relations. Harvard's program has a well-deserved reputation for excellence. In addition to the vast resources of the university, doctoral students have the unique opportunity to live in Harvard's Center for the Study of World Religions. This setting fosters daily interaction with other doctoral students of various religious backgrounds, Harvard faculty, and visiting scholars from all over the world. For me, the Center provided a congenial context to pursue my concerns academically and experientially.

In the midst of doctoral studies a dramatic international event captured the attention of the world media: student militants seized the U.S. embassy compound in Tehran and held 53 Americans hostage. From the outset, the Iranian government indicated its interest in meeting with representatives of the religious community rather than U.S. government officials. Through an unusual series of events, I was one of seven people invited to Iran in December 1979. Our religiously-based delegation sought to facilitate communication and encourage a nonviolent resolution to the hostage conflict. As one of the two clergy in the group who had studied the Qur'an and the Islamic religious tradition, I was warmly received by many Iranian religious and political leaders.

On two other occasions (in 1980 and 1981), I and a colleague were invited back to Iran as "honest American ministers" who could help facilitate communication where little was taking place. These efforts attracted considerable attention in the international media since we were among the only Americans involved in personal meetings with Ayatollah Khomeini, then-President Bani-Sadr, Ali Akbar Hashemi ar-Rafsanjani, the speaker of the parliament, as well as various other political and religious leaders. On each visit, we spent several hours meeting with the students occupying the U.S. embassy compound. A number of Muslim leaders in the U.S. and in the Middle East knew of these efforts and were supportive of them.

From December 1979 until the middle of 1981, I took a leave from dissertation work in order to concentrate on the issues surrounding the hostage conflict. During those months, I wrote a number of background and op-ed articles for major publications, appeared frequently on national and local television and radio programs, and travelled throughout the country lecturing in colleges, universities, seminaries, conferences, churches, and synagogues.

One overriding impression from the unique vantage point afforded by those various endeavors spanning eighteen months centers on the pervasive ignorance and deep bias most Americans exhibited concerning Islam and the forces at work within many predominantly Muslim societies. This dynamic was (and is) all the more striking — and disturbing — in view of the size and importance of Muslim communities in the contemporary world. The experiences related to my direct involvement in the Iran hostage conflict underscored the importance of the fair-minded study of other traditions and theological reflection related to religious pluralism; it also confirmed the centrality of interreligious understanding and cooperation as pragmatic necessities in our increasingly fragile and interconnected world.

In 1982, I began work as the Director of Interfaith Programs for the Fellowship of Reconciliation, an international organization committed to nonviolent conflict resolution. Two years later, I assumed responsibilities as the Director for the Middle East Office for the National Council of Churches (NCC). My work at the NCC continued for seven years. Both of these positions have required extensive international and domestic travel related, in part, to programmatic work in the interfaith arena. A major focus of my efforts in the United States has centered on education — writing, lecturing, leading conferences — related to the contemporary Middle East, Islam, and Jewish-Christian-Muslim relations. Between 1977 and 1990, I have traveled to various parts of the Middle East on more than 30 different occasions, ranging from one week to two months. In 1977–78, my spouse and I lived in Egypt and traveled widely throughout the region.

These various experiences have provided extraordinary learning opportunities. In the course of the past fifteen years, my academic, experiential, and personal concerns related to pluralism have been challenged, refined, developed, and reshaped. The fundamental convictions, however, remain: the study of and engagement with people of other religious traditions is a central priority both for Christian theological reflection and for the practical issues confronting all of us who share this planet. In a way heretofore unknown, interreligious understanding and cooperation are vital to the future of the human family. The consequences of actions among people and nations who see one another primarily through the lens of ignorance and/or prejudice may threaten the very survival of the planet.

My experience with numerous church-related groups and world affairs organizations around the United States has served to confirm this perspective. It has also made clear the paucity of material available to assist interested non-specialists. While a number of articles, monographs, and books have been published on Islam and contemporary political developments during the past decade, most of these materials remain largely inaccessible. This book represents an effort to help fill that gap. My purpose is to provide a text for interested individuals, church study groups, seminary students, and others who recognize the importance of Christian-Muslim understanding and cooperation but need resources to facilitate constructive engagement with the issues.

The primary audience addressed in the book is the Christian community in the West. The text invites readers to reflect in new ways on the obstacles and opportunities in contemporary Christian-Muslim relations. For Christians, this process involves an examination of the images, fears, and stereotypes that permeate Western views on Islam. In fact, most of us need to "unlearn" what we have been taught overtly—or more often, subtly—through our cultural heritage. Thus, the first chapter focusses on the importance of contemporary Christian-Muslim relations and the obstacles blocking many Western Christians from a constructive study of Islam and engagement of interfaith issues.

The next two chapters seek to provide the context within which the challenges and opportunities can be positively addressed. Chapter two describes the fundamental tenets of the Islamic religious tradition. Here, as elsewhere in the text, selected use of footnotes provides the reader with an annotated bibliography for further study. With a clearer understanding of Islam in mind, the third chapter surveys the history of Christian-Muslim understanding of one another. In this process, we are better able to see how and why the relationships have been predominantly characterized by mistrust, misunderstanding, and mutual antipathy.

The fourth chapter challenges us to consider again the biblical bases for Christian understanding of and relations with people outside the visible walls of the Church. In the process of thinking self-critically about our perspectives, it is helpful to know what other options might be available. Thus, the chapter also identifies several ways in which contemporary theologians are wrestling with the meaning of religious pluralism.

The fifth chapter examines the Christian-Muslim "dialogue movement," particularly as it has been fostered through the Vatican and the World Council of Churches during the second half of this century. These structured initiatives constitute a primary way in which Christians have sought to engage Muslim neighbors in the search for a more constructive and cooperative future. The dialogue movement has remained a surprisingly well-kept secret, even in the very churches comprising the constituency for these world bodies.

Finally, we move beyond dialogue to consider other opportunities for building Christian-Muslim relations. While there are no easy answers or simple solutions, there are ways to move forward into a future characterized by mutual respect and cooperation. This chapter challenges Christians to move into that future with courage, creativity, and openness.

In their respective self-understanding, Christians and Muslims endeavor both to understand and to live their lives in accordance with the will of God. It is a task far easier said than done. The New Testament and the Qur'an both enjoin the faithful to maintain a continual internal struggle with the human frailties and selfish desires that hinder us from identifying and following the will of God. In Islam, this great, ongoing struggle within oneself for moral perfection is known as *jihad* ("strenuous effort" or "striving in the way of God"). The secondary emphasis on *jihad* as outward struggle in the name of God—particularly in the context of military confrontation—has received considerable attention in the Western media as several extremist groups have employed the term *jihad* (e.g., "Islamic Jihad," usually translated "Islamic Holy War"). This negative, violent emphasis has overshadowed the rich and positive primary meaning of the term.

The challenge presented to Christians and Muslims today

moves beyond the individual life of faith. We must either find new ways to live together or we may not live at all on this planet. The focus of this text is on Christian understanding of Islam and responsibility in interfaith relations. Ultimately, the strength and vitality of Christian-Muslim relations depends on the attitudes, intentions, and behavior of both partners. The title of the book, *Striving Together*, alludes both to the difficulty and the shared responsibility for the venture.

As with any book drawing upon experiences and insights over a period of years, there are many people who have contributed substantially to my understanding and deserve recognition. My indebtedness to some is reflected in the text and notes; many others—ranging from seminary and graduate school friends and professors to individual acquaintances who shared a cup of coffee and conversation in Cairo, Jerusalem, or Dallas—will not be so readily apparent. Several people among those unnamed above have also made valuable suggestions in the process of refining this present text. In particular, I am grateful to the following people for their critical comments and editorial suggestions: Daud Assad, Dale Bishop, John Borelli, Elias Mallon, Fr. Tom Michel, Tariq Mitri, Dick Mulder, Muzammil Siddiqi, Maurice Smith, Peggy Thomas, and Hans Ucco. Robert Ellsberg, editor for this book, has provided both the critical reflection and personal encouragement necessary at each step in the process. He and a host of people on the staff of Orbis Books have engaged their professional tasks with the kind of congenial personal interaction that made pleasurable even the more tedious aspects of producing a book. Finally, a word of appreciation to my spouse, Nancy. In addition to her own career as an occupational therapist and the innumerable responsibilities of a mother with two small children, she has constantly supported and encouraged my work. Through the rigors of two graduate schools, frequent travel, and many hours that found me ensconced in the study, she has been the friend, critic, and confidante one can only hope to have in a spouse. With love and appreciation this book is dedicated to her.

STRIVING TOGETHER

CHAPTER ONE

Obstacles and Opportunities in Christian-Muslim Relations

In the early morning hours of January 1, 1980, I sat with six other American clergy in a small room deep inside the U.S. embassy compound in Tehran. Having already met with many of the top religious and political leaders in the country, we were invited to meet with the Iranian student militants who had seized the U.S. embassy two months earlier and were still holding 53 Americans captive. About two hours into the wide-ranging discussion with their leaders, one of the students declared, "The taking and holding of these spies is a great Islamic act!" To the mild surprise of several of my colleagues, I immediately replied, "That is nonsense."

The student looked at me and, after a moment, asked what I meant. My response: "I think I understand your political motivations for seizing this embassy and holding people hostage. You have made clear your anger and frustration with U.S. intervention in Iran over the years. Given this history, I can well understand why you fear a possible U.S. military effort to reinstate the Shah [who was in the United States at the time]. Even so, you must know that your actions here are not only illegal, they are immoral. And, they are certainly not Islamic. Your responsibility as Muslims is to protect the foreigner in your midst. Although a few of the embassy personnel may have some connection to U.S. intelligence gathering activities [what embassy doesn't? And, Tehran was known as the center of U.S. intelligence activity in the region], the overwhelming majority are surely not spies. While I strongly disagree with what you are doing and believe it ultimately will hurt, not further, the image and understanding of Islam in the world, I must also say that your rhetoric is far from helpful. To call hostages 'spies' and declare your actions Islamic in no way helps you protect or further the fragile process of your revolution."

After a longer pause, the student said softly, "What we are doing may not be Islamic, but it is revolutionary!"

Through this type of direct, honest exchange, a few of us were able to engage the students and Iranian leaders in productive and respectful ways. We were able to help open channels of communication. As one student put it when two of us were invited back six months later, "We trust you. You have studied Islam. You are not afraid of us; you know that we are not crazy murderers. We take you seriously as 'honest Americans' because you have taken us seriously as human beings long before there was a revolution or the takeover of the embassy."

For nearly two years, the U.S. and other media provided the world with unprecedented coverage of the Iranian hostage conflict. It was the media event of the decade, if not several decades; a veritable three-ring circus. On my first trip to Iran I was particularly struck by the presence of three times as many Western journalists covering the events from just outside the embassy gates as there were hostages within the compound.

In the midst of the "coverage" there were many articles, as well as television and radio programs, offering substantive information which helped make sense of the conflict in light of political, economic, military, and religious history. Unfortunately, the vast majority of Americans either did not have easy access to or make an effort to process this type of information. Rather, it was the daily barrage of images on American television that informed the thinking of most. For those of us who lived through these events, images of irrational mobs, sinister terrorist figures, and defiant, bloodthirsty Muslim leaders remain vivid.

Without question, the Iranian revolution was a watershed event. In an overwhelmingly popular uprising, Iranians sent a brutal and unrepresentative regime packing. Viewed from the perspective of the post World War II political status quo, this event was an unmistakable harbinger of a new day. From the perspective of many poor, disenfranchised, and oppressed people around the world, the message was quite different: they, too, need not languish under repressive governments which serve as uncritical allies of or client states for world powers.

It is also clear that Islamic institutions and Muslims motivated by their faith are playing an increasingly central role in a variety of countries in transition to new political structures. A wide disparity exists, however, in the Western understanding of Islam and the strong, frequently turbulent forces at work within the Muslim world today. It makes all the difference if one begins by recognizing that the world's political order is necessarily changing and new forces (including Muslims inspired by their religious tradition) are at work in the process or, instead, one begins with the assumption that Islam itself is a problem that threatens stability and order in the world.

The media coverage of the Iranian hostage conflict served to reinforce the latter assumption.[1] In the process, a longstanding stereotype in the West[2] was perpetuated, namely: Islam is inherently intolerant, fanatic, violent, and menacing. This image of Islam differs dramatically from its historical reality as a dynamic tradition, inspiring and nurturing hundreds of millions of adherents for centuries. To understand the difference between Islam as a complex, living religious tradition and the stereotypical images of Islam (particularly in the West) is the critical point of departure for those who wish to pursue a more constructive future in Christian-Muslim relations.

In the decade following the Iran hostage situation, various developments in predominantly Muslim societies have continued to occupy center stage in international news. Media attention, with rare exceptions, inevitably concentrates on dramatic or sensational events. Never mind that the overwhelming majority of Muslims are horrified by a Lebanese truck bomber acting in the name of Islam, the negative image of Islam is perpetuated by the extremist, misguided actions of individuals and groups. Sadly, such behavior is a familiar component in the respective histories of both Christians and Muslims. But, the chilling examples of violence, even slaughter, in the name of God should not be equated with the religious traditions, even if the perpetrators claim to take inspiration from their faith. Such individuals and groups comprise a part of the mosaic, but they are surely not representative of the moral and ethical teachings of the larger religious communities, both of which have stood well the test of time.

There was a new twist with the 1989 publication of Salman Rushdie's highly controversial novel, *The Satanic Verses*. The book touched off a volatile, multi-sided debate around the world. For several months, political and religious leaders, writers, publishers and journalists, among others, declared their positions on the offensive passages in the book and the inherent conflict between freedom of speech and religious sensitivities. The text was banned in India, Bangladesh, Egypt, and Saudi Arabia; it set off riots in Pakistan; it was burned by angry demonstrators in England; and, it was pulled from many bookstores in the United States.

The episode became a full-blown media event when the then-head of state in Iran, the Ayatollah Khomeini, declared that Rushdie must die for his blasphemy. What should be done in response to this decree? By whom should action be taken? On what bases were governmental decisions (in Great Britain and elsewhere) to be made? Traditional international boundaries and legal jurisdictions were blurred by the death sentence from afar and the declared willingness of a few zealots in London to carry out the assassination should they have an opportunity.

There were many different facets visible in the Rushdie incident. The issues were often confused, in part by people with differing motives. Some Muslim leaders deliberately manipulated and exacerbated the controversy as a means for gaining domestic political advantage in their respective settings; on the other side, it appeared that some of the most vocal advocates of freedom of expression exploited this episode as a timely and useful platform for self-promotion, while others simply seized the moment to denigrate Islam.

After reading the novel and meeting with many Muslims in the United States and the Middle East who were knowledgeable of the text, it is obvious why virtually all Muslims would declare the most controversial sections deeply offensive or blasphemous.

The book presents a thinly veiled representation of the prophet Muhammad, the Qur'an, and the process of divine revelation of the scriptures in ways that are guaranteed to offend. Add to this the apparent depiction of Muhammad's wives as prostitutes and it becomes clear why most Muslims were unimpressed by Rushdie's claim that "the book is not about Islam, but about migration, metamorphosis, divided selves, love, death, London and Bombay."[3]

Regretably, but predictably, the intense media attention during the Rushdie affair focussed on extremist positions among Muslims. The fact that most Muslims, while deeply offended, would not concur with Khomeini's decision seemed lost in the process. One of the most revered spiritual leaders among Sunni Muslims, the Shaikh of al-Azhar in Cairo, publicly disagreed with Khomeini's pronouncement. Other leaders echoed this sentiment, reflecting both the diversity and the diffuse nature of authority within the Islamic world. Even so, in the Western media, the most extreme position was generally portrayed as the norm.

Among U.S. Christian leaders, however, there were notable, if subtle, shifts in response to the Rushdie incident as compared with earlier international issues related to the Muslim world. More sensitivity, born out of personal interaction with Muslims, was in evidence than had been visible earlier. New York's Cardinal John O'Connor declared the text offensive and urged Catholics neither to buy nor read the book. Protestant and Orthodox ecumenical representatives issued a measured statement through the National Council of Churches' Office on Christian-Muslim Relations. In it, they empathized with Muslim sentiment, affirmed the principle of freedom of expression and cautioned against overreaction on all sides. Prominent fundamentalist leaders said little about Muslim sensitivities. They seemed most concerned to differentiate between Muslim behavior (epitomized by Khomeini's pronouncement) and their own campaigns and protestations, such as the outcry over Martin Scorcese's film, "The Last Temptation of Christ."

THE CHALLENGE OF GLOBAL INTERDEPENDENCE

The issues surrounding the highly charged Rushdie controversy were never clearly resolved. Even so, the events did help to focus collective attention on new dynamics in the global village. While the world has always been religiously diverse, the self-conscious awareness of pluralism is no longer linked primarily to those who happen to live in close proximity. The ramifications of various expressions of heartfelt concerns, within the Muslim community in this instance, are felt all over the world. The world itself is one neighborhood. One has only to turn on the television to be in touch instantly with people and events in Latin America, Eastern Europe, the Middle East, Southern Africa, and China.

Through modern communications, international travel, and the growing influence of multinational corporations, we are all connected.

The challenges presented by this new situation are many and complex. The Rushdie affair vividly reminds us yet again that religious, ethnic, and cultural diversity are crucial and sometimes volatile ingredients in the global mix. Other prominent examples in the late 1980s were evident in fierce conflicts in Lebanon, Sudan, India, Sri Lanka, and Soviet Azerbaijan. Almost without exception such local or regional conflicts are not defined strictly by religious differences. Perceptions of political and economic injustice as well as social and cultural factors are often at the root of conflict.

Unlike the past, however, the particularities of regional disputes can no longer be isolated from the larger human community. Local conflicts move out into the international domain through instantaneous media coverage, the actions by partisans outside the immediate vicinity and the inevitable direct or indirect intervention by regional or superpowers. In a very real sense, most conflicts reflect in microcosm the complexity and linkages in our world today.

In the final decade of the twentieth century the more than five billion inhabitants of our planet are joined together through political, economic, and ecological interdependence in unprecedented ways. A few examples illustrate the point.

The August 1990 Iraqi invasion of Kuwait provoked an immediate response in the world community. The prospect of disruption in the flow of oil from the Persian/Arabia gulf sent shock waves throughout global markets. Oil prices soared; stock markets in Tokyo, New York, London, Bonn and Sydney reacted daily for many weeks in response to news from the gulf. These economic indicators as well as the U.S. led multinational military response to the invasion were dramatic reminders of the interdependent nature of the global community.

The 1988 nuclear accident at Chernobyl was not only a catastrophe for Soviet citizens living nearby. Medium and longterm consequences will continue to affect the international community for years to come. Similarly, the depletion of the protective ozone layer in the earth's atmosphere, pollution of the oceans, and the impact of destroying portions of the Brazilian rain forests are global concerns.

Numerous urgent political and humanitarian issues challenge the collective wisdom in the human family. Meaningful progress in the complicated and daunting search for peace and social justice, the safeguarding of human rights, the plight of refugees, endemic hunger and poverty issues will require the concerted and cooperative efforts of the international community. These tasks may be complicated or facilitated by the rapidly changing political linkages among Western democracies, the former socialist states in Eastern Europe and various countries in the developing world. An even greater political and economic interdependence will undoubtedly characterize the new relationships in the 1990s and beyond.

The recognition of and initial efforts to address issues of political, economic, and ecological interdependence have not been matched by concurrent efforts to facilitate understanding and cooperation across religious and cultural lines. Yet, it is undeniably true that the numerous challenges posed by global interdependence are now and will continue to be complicated by religious and cultural diversity. Nowhere is the agenda more urgent than with the adherents of the two largest religious traditions: Christians and Muslims. Together, these two communities of faith encompass nearly half of the world's population. Both communities are present in all parts of the world and both are growing rapidly. Without question, the ways in which Christians and Muslims relate and interact will shape the future of this planet — for better or worse.

At the beginning of the 1990s, Muslims number between 900

million and 1.2 billion. Contrary to the popular image in the West, the large majority of Muslims do not live in the Middle East. Indonesia has the largest Muslim population with more than 150 million adherents; India's Muslim community, although a minority, numbers 120 million; Pakistan and Bangladesh follow with roughly 100 and 92 million, respectively; Turkey is home to approximately 48 million; and Egypt, by far the largest Arabic-speaking Middle Eastern country, totals some 45 million. In 60 countries Muslims comprise the majority; in another 15 nations Muslims constitute a substantial minority, ranging from 15-49% of the population; and in 22 countries they represent less than 15% of the total.[4]

Even these smaller minority communities can be very substantial. In China, for instance, where Muslims are less than 3% of the population, they number between 25 and 30 million. Similarly, the southern tier of the U.S.S.R. includes more than 40 million Muslims.

Although accurate figures are not easy to ascertain, there are well over four million Muslims in the United States.[5]

Demographers predict a rapid growth in the American Muslim community during the coming two decades. In the early years of next century, Muslims will surpass Jews as the second largest religious community in the United States. In Europe, Islam is already the second largest religious tradition, collectively and in virtually every country.

From a purely pragmatic standpoint, the pressing issues facing the interdependent international community and the growth of Islam in the West should stimulate North Americans and Europeans to review and reconsider their understanding of Islam and relationships with Muslims as neighbors and citizens in our pluralistic societies. My personal efforts to impress this point on leaders of the U.S. Congress has had mixed results.

In the spring of 1984, for example, during the throes of the U.S. presidential primary campaign, several politicians proposed that the U.S. should move its embassy in Israel from Tel Aviv to Jerusalem. The Reagan Administration, upholding more than forty years of U.S. policy, opposed this initiative. In the Congressional hearings, I was among those invited to speak to the question. The intensity of election-year politics combined with emotional attachment to Israel made this a very hot issue. During the course of questions and answers after the formal testimony (which ran for over three hours on national cable television), I made the point that the fledgling peace process in the Middle East would not be served by precipitous U.S. action, particularly when it was certain to provoke a strong response from Muslims all the way from Morocco to the Philippines. After reiterating the importance of Jerusalem for Muslims, I suggested that members of Congress would do well to learn more of the Islamic world and of the forces at work within many predominantly Muslim societies. Failure to do so would assure further serious mistakes, at the very least, in U.S. policy and diplomacy during this time of rapidly changing political world order.

One Congressman, Rep. Larry Smith from Florida, responded immediately to my comment, saying, "You imply that there has been a lack of accurate information about Islam. I cannot think of examples where this Congress has been so uninformed. Can you?"

In response, I put the question back to the Congressman. "Do you recall President Carter toasting the Shah of Iran on New Year's Eve in 1977, calling him 'a leader greatly loved by his people' and calling Iran an 'island of stability in the sea of chaos in the Middle East'? Less than a year later the Shah was hounded from the Peacock Throne by a broad-based, popular revolution. Would you argue, Congressman, that this public statement or the political actions taken by the U.S. government before and during the Iranian revolution reflected a correct understanding of the forces at work within that predominantly Muslim society?"

After agreeing I had a point, he then wondered whether I could think of any other examples. "How about Lebanon?" I asked. "Surely you would not argue that the decision to send U.S. marines into Lebanon in 1982 as a peacekeeping force and the policy decisions taken during the disastrous months they were there reflected a correct understanding of the dynamics — particularly among Shi'ite Muslims — in Lebanon." After a brief silence, the Congressman changed the subject.

CHRISTIAN RESPONSIBILITY AND THEOLOGICAL INQUIRY

Another set of compelling reasons for pursuing an accurate understanding of Islam relates to Christian responsibility and self-understanding. Christian responsibility in relationship with others is clearly stated in the biblical text: "You shall not bear false witness against your neighbor" (Ex 20:16); "Love your neighbor as yourself" (Lv 19:18; Mt 19:19; Gal 5:14); and, "If it is possible, so far as it depends upon you, live peaceably with all" (Rom 12:18). How is it possible to avoid bearing false witness against, or to love one's neighbor, or live together in peace if we know so little about our neighbor? Even worse, how is it possible to live in faithfulness to these biblical imperatives when much of what we think we know is incorrect?

Contemporary Christian theological reflection provides further impetus for understanding Islam and other religious traditions more accurately. Increasingly, Christian theologians are regarding issues of pluralism and religious diversity as vital to an adequate self-understanding. From the inception of the church, Christians have been aware of religious diversity and have interacted with people and ideas from other religious traditions. The New Testament records details of Christian communities struggling with their relationships and identity vis-à-vis the Jewish tradition, from which most of the early followers of Jesus had come. The biblical record also presents issues debated by first-century Christians as they encountered pagan religious practices throughout the Roman Empire. Church history—or, for that matter, the history of any major religious tradition—records various ways in which people of faith have endeavored to understand, respond to, convert or, far too often, eradicate those who did not share the same worldview.

Several factors have converged to make Christian theological reflection on pluralism a primary focus in the second half of the twentieth century. Extensive global interaction and more accurate knowledge of other religious traditions have helped remove obstacles generated by partial or distorted information. Moreover, scholarly insights into the dynamic, relational, and deabsolutized notion of "truth" have necessitated a reexamination of the meaning of absolute, static, propositional truth claims.[6]

At the same time, fresh study of the Bible and major interpreters of the faith in church history have revealed a more complex picture than most people have assumed.

How are we to understand, interpret, and live out the particularity of Christian faith as understood through God's revelation and activity in Jesus Christ in our pluralistic world? Is it possible to understand God's presence and love for creation in ways that expand traditional, exclusivist theology? What can we learn from biblical, historical, and experiential sources as we reflect anew on our theological frame of reference? More particularly, how can we understand Islam as a post-Christian religious tradition? What are the implications for evangelization? for mission? for *diakonia*, or service ministries? These and related questions are of paramount importance for Christians—and, I would argue, for Jews, Muslims, Hindus, Buddhists, and others. Self-understanding in relation to those who do not share the same worldview but do share the same fragile planet bears directly on behavior and action.

These are weighty questions for which simplistic answers will not suffice. We will not resolve the questions in this present text; nor is it likely that Christians will widely embrace definitive answers in the near future. However, responsible people of faith can—and must—identify and pursue the right questions. A fresh look at the biblical record and a survey of some of the creative perspectives being articulated by Christian scholars today can provide helpful parameters within which Christians might move forward in pursuit of these imposing questions.

WHERE TO BEGIN?

An ancient and famous Chinese proverb declares, "A journey of one thousand *li* (miles) begins with the first step." This simple, yet helpful proverb needs a minor modification in the present instance. As we begin the journey toward a better understanding of Islam, we must start with a step backwards. Christians in the West bring a good deal more baggage with them to the point of departure than most of us realize. There is a long history of interaction between Christians and Muslims—from the rise and spread of Islam, through the period of the Crusades, up to the present time. Western views of Islam have been shaped, perpetuated, and transmitted through these encounters, through literature and, more subtly, through our cultural heritage. A better, more precise knowledge of this history—the subject of chapter three below—is necessary if we hope to fashion more constructive relations in the future.

Although contemporary Western civilization has been shaped by the Judeo-Christian-Islamic tradition, remarkably few people recognize the positive and decisive contributions from the latter of the three great monotheistic communities of faith. Rather, the prevalent images and perceptions of Islam have been formed in the context of fear, prejudice, and hostility. Contemporary manifestations were highlighted earlier in relation to the Iran hostage conflict and the Rushdie affair. The first step on the journey, therefore, must be a step back; we must begin with a self-critical reflection of the baggage we carry—wittingly or unwittingly.

The majority Christian—and particularly white Christian—community is aided in this process by the significant progress in Jewish-Christian relations and in the struggle to eradicate racial discrimination. The depth and pervasiveness of Western Christian antisemitism was manifest in the unspeakable horror of the Holocaust. In the half-century following the systematic destruction of over six million Jews, many Christians have become sensitized to the long history of antisemitism and its destructive manifestations. While few people overtly display a racist stance, it is increasingly clear that an anti-Jewish bias remains a persistent component of the Western Christian heritage. Happily, concerted educational efforts, structured dialogue meetings, and cooperative Jewish-Christian institutional initiatives have engendered new awareness and sensitivity in recent decades. The slow and painful process of education is underway.

Similarly, the civil rights movement provided a teachable moment. The history of black-white relations in the United States is well known. Through the courageous struggle for civil rights and racial equality, black (as well as many white, Jewish, and others) American leaders challenged the structural racism throughout the institutions of society. In the process, many thoughtful, fairminded white Americans have discoverd the sinister and pervasive nature of racism. People who never perceived of themselves as racist have had to acknowledge the need to "unlearn" what had been taught or transmitted subtly through the value systems of the predominantly white Christian society.

The process of self-critical reflection and "unlearning," the step back, has barely commenced in relation to Islam, Arabs, and Muslims. The fact that these three distinctive terms are used almost interchangeably in popular usage speaks to the point. That Islam, the religious tradition, and Muslims, the adherents, are not identical with Arabic-speaking Middle Eastern people has somehow eluded popular discovery. Relatively few Americans, for instance, recognize the distinctive presence and contribution of the 10–12 million Arabs who are indigenous Christians. Although they comprise approximately 10% of the Arab world, Christians are a substantial minority. To put the numbers in perspective, it is striking to realize that there are three times as many indigenous Christians in the Middle East as there are Jews in Israel. That Arab Christians are almost invisible in the West (with the notable exception of news reports about "Christian" militias fighting "Muslim" militias in Lebanon) is all the more remarkable since these communities have been present in and near the Holy Land since the beginning of the church.

Unlike those working on Jewish-Christian relations and civil rights issues, the voices of those who challenge the stereotypical and racist images of Islam, Arabs, and Muslims have remained almost inaudible in the society at large. How widespread is the anti-Islamic, anti-Arab, anti-Muslim bias? Consider the following.

During the 1970s, the U.S. Federal Bureau of Investigation conducted an elaborate "sting" operation designed to expose corrupt government officials willing to use their influence and power in exchange for cash payments. The ploy involved FBI agents disguised as Arab sheikhs who approached officials in order to buy favors. The operation was named ABSCAM, short for Arab Scam. When the sting operation worked and a number of major figures — including a Senator and several Congressional Representatives — were videotaped accepting bribes, ABSCAM drew national media attention. For months, news stories focussed on various dimensions of the operation, the indictments, the trials, and so forth. Throughout the process, almost no one apart from a few Arab-American organizations protested the derogatory, offensive caricature of Arabs. It simply didn't occur to people in the FBI or in the media that there was anything wrong with an FBI operation representing Arabs as extremely rich and unscrupulous, or linking "Arab" and "scam" in its name.

When using this illustration in public presentations, not everyone immediately sees the problem. The light comes on, however, when the question is asked: Can you imagine an officially sanctioned FBI operation being called "JEWSCAM" or "BLACKSCAM"? Can you imagine the swift and strong protest from Jews, blacks, other minority groups and many white Americans who would immediately see the negative, offensive, and unacceptable caricature conveyed in the very title of the program? The protesters would be absolutely right to challenge the bias, even racism, implicit in such an operation. But where was the outcry, the protest over the name ABSCAM or the depiction of Arabs?

No less a figure than the President of the United States, Ronald Reagan, publicly employed sweeping and highly negative generalizations when, in January 1981, he depicted Iranians as "barbarians." Various Congressional and other governmental leaders periodically vented their frustrations over events involving Americans in Lebanon and Libya during the 1980s with similar caricatures of Arabs. Listen carefully to the references, the casual use of stereotypes when Middle Eastern Muslims or Arabs figure prominently into the news. Then ask, where is the outcry? Who is protesting the dehumanizing characterization of Arabs, Iranians, and Muslims?

Jack Shaheen, a professor of mass communications at Southern Illinois University, has monitored and written about the popular stereotyping of Arabs in major media during the 1980s. In 1986, he published a study of nineteen major motion pictures which featured portrayals of Arabs. Shaheen documents "a disturbing recurrence of similarly negative characters, with inaccurate and stereotypical settings." Noting three exceptions where there is some balance in the images projected, he summarizes the major findings with these words:

> The Arab male is portrayed as a contemptible character—cowardly, primitive, ignorant, cruel, vicious, lecherous and

fabulously wealthy. An Arab woman is either a sensuous belly dancer, whore, terrorist, or a veiled, silent appendage to her husband.

Filmmakers too often dip into their script bag for the "Instant Arab Kit." For women, it contains belly dancers' outfits and veils; for the men, it consists of *kuffiyahs*, flowing robes, sunglasses, scimitars, limousines and camels. Oil wells, sand dunes and souks provide the background.[7]

Like the movies, the visual images conveyed by television are powerful and formative. Shaheen's more extensive study, *The TV Arab*, posits essentially the same conclusions as above.[8] Laurence Michalak, a cultural anthropologist at the University of California in Berkeley, documents similar findings in a booklet surveying images of Arabs in songs, jokes, political cartoons, comics, movies and television.[9]

There have been positive images of Arabs and Muslims as well. The name of Anwar Sadat still evokes a favorable response among most Americans. But even in the case of the former Egyptian president, the picture is complex. Usually described as a "moderate" Arab leader, Sadat was infrequently portrayed as an Arabic-speaking Middle Eastern Muslim. Rather, he was a courageous, tough-minded leader who understood and played well the international political game. The fact that he came into American homes (via television) wearing a suit and tie and speaking English significantly enhanced his ability to penetrate the unconscious bias against Arabs and Muslims.

The effort to understand the Islamic tradition begins with a step backward in order to know better the influences and perspectives already present by virtue of one's heritage and present-day cultural influences.

VALUE JUDGMENTS AND REAL DIFFERENCES

Historians of religion frequently advocate restraint or refraining from judgment as a guiding principle in the study of religious traditions. In order to comprehend what Islam is and means to Muslims, we must refrain from evaluating the truth or value of particular elements within the tradition on the basis of our own religious experience. Insofar as possible, we should strive to let the Qur'an and Muslims speak for themselves. Or, as is the case with this book, when a non-Muslim writes about Islam, it should be done in such a way that Muslims recognize themselves in the description.

The positive side of this effort to refrain from judgment is empathetic understanding. In this sense, we should draw upon our religious background and experience, not to judge, but to understand. A description of various types of prayer or fasting or celebration of holy days in Islam, for instance, can be more readily understood in relation to parallel practices and concepts in one's own tradition.

The effort to understand does not require that one never evaluate or make judgments. The example of my encounter with the Iranian students at the outset of this chapter is a case in point. While I understood their motivations, hopes, and fears (insofar as it is possible from the outside), I strongly disagreed with the tactics they employed — not only seizing an embassy and holding hostages, but also attempting to justify their actions as Islamic.

There are real and substantial differences between Christians and Muslims. Fundamental disagreements exist, for example, in the respective theological views on the nature and efficacy of Jesus' life, death and resurrection. In the political realm, wide disparity is evident when adherents advocate theoretical understandings of the role of their religious tradition in shaping and governing contemporary nation-states. These and other points where minor or radically different positions exist should, by no means, be pushed aside or glossed over. Muslims and Christians must each deal openly with such matters of concern. The challenge and requirement for both communities is to engage one another honestly and in the light of accurate information. The bias and misinformation permeating the history of relations between the world's two largest religious traditions must be understood and overcome. But overcoming prejudices does not mean Christians and Muslims will resolve the deep differences that separate them.

The overused American saying, "Before you judge someone, walk a mile in his or her shoes," is apt. The goal, initially, is to try and grasp how the world looks from the perspective of another. This is not to imply that the world looks the same to hundreds of millions of Muslims. On the contrary, diversity within Islam is as rich as within the Christian community. Religious traditions are anything but static. However, as with the Christian tradition, there are common threads, basic elements that comprise the context within which a more accurate and sophisticated picture can be drawn.

Our effort here is to provide that context in the hope that better understanding will contribute substantially to the practical and theological agenda near the turn of the twenty-first century. We hope to facilitate communication and cooperation among the adherents in the world's two largest religious communities. The challenge of global interdependence demands no less. We trust, furthermore, that a more accurate understanding of Islam will be invaluable grist for the theological mill as Christians wrestle with the meaning and consequences of particularity and pluralism.

CHAPTER TWO

Toward Understanding Islam

Unlike many religious traditions which evolved slowly from relatively obscure origins, Islam appeared in the full light of history. From modest origins in seventh-century Arabia, it burst onto the scene and spread rapidly northward into the Fertile Crescent, west across North Africa and east through the ancient lands of the Tigris and Euphrates valley into central Asia. Within a century, the domain of Islam stretched from southern Spain to the northwest portion of India.

The unparalleled success in this phenomenal growth was due in part to the zealous faith and military prowess of the first generations of Arab Muslims, as well as the decadent state of the Mediterranean world. The continuing durability and strength of Islam, however, is a testimony to its clear and positive message. The simple confession of faith, "There is no god but God, and Muhammad is the messenger of God," reflects the central tenets of Islam: There is one true God, Creator and Sustainer of the universe; and, God's will has been manifest through prophetic revelation. Muslims affirm that this revelation is now contained in the Qur'an, the literal, perfect, and complete word of God. Muhammad was chosen by God to be the instrument through which the final revelation was given. The proper human response is obedience to God not only in worship but in all aspects of life.

A brief Arabic lesson helps to demystify the fundamental meaning of key terms and make clear the basic orientation of

Muslims. Like Hebrew, Arabic is built on a consonantal root-system. Most words are derived from three consonants which convey a basic notion. The letters **k-t-b,** for instance, relate to the idea of writing. When different vowels, prefixes or suffixes are added, words are formed. Thus, **kataba** means "he wrote"; a **kitab** is a "book"; a **maktab** is an "office" (a place where writing occurs); a **maktabah** is a "library," and so forth. The root meanings of **s-l-m** have to do with submission to the will of God and peace. Three familiar words derive from this root: **salam, Islam** and **Muslim.** "Salam" means "peace, well-being"; it originates from the same root as the more familiar Hebrew word *shalom* (The "s" and "sh" are distinctive letters in Arabic and Hebrew; they are often transposed in usage in the two languages.) Islam means "submission to the will of God"; it is "the religion of peace." Those who submit themselves in obedience to God are Muslims; they are, by definition, people "at peace" in creation.

Muslims worship the same God as Christians and Jews. Many non-Arabic speakers, confused by the name Allah, have not made this connection. Allah is simply the Arabic term for God. Arabic-speaking Christians pray to Allah, just as the French pray to *Dieu* and Germans to *Gott.* For Muslims there is no ambiguity; the One, true God is the God of Abraham, Moses, Jesus, and Muhammad.

As with the Christian religious tradition, foundational doctrines and devotional practices in Islam can be described generally in a relatively straightforward manner. The vitality of the religious tradition as embraced and lived out by faithful adherents is a far more complex and subtle matter. Christians, for example, believe that Jesus, the incarnation of God, died for the sins of the world and was resurrected miraculously by God. These affirmations provide little indication, however, of how people of faith have, in different times and places, appropriated the implications of Jesus' life, death, and resurrection. The same is true for Islam. Descriptive accounts of basic teachings fail to convey the rich texture and diversity found within the history of this extensive religious tradition.

In this chapter, we seek only to provide an orientation to

some of the major elements that provide the framework for Islam.[1]

This is a necessary first step in the process of developing a new, more accurate understanding. But, it is only the first step. Detailed knowledge requires an investment of considerable time and energy in order to work through what Clifford Geertz calls "the dense thicket of the particulars."[2]

THE ROLE AND IMPORTANCE OF MUHAMMAD

Muhammad was born in 570 C.E. in Mecca. He was raised by members of his extended family since his father had died prior to his birth and his mother passed away when he was six. From age eight he lived with his uncle, Abu Talib. Mecca was a commercial center, a crossroads on the trade routes across the vast expanse of Arabia. Muhammad, who learned the caravan business from his uncle, proved adept in business. His reputation for honesty is reflected in the honorific name by which he was known: *al-amin* ("the honest one"). At age 25, he married a wealthy caravan owner, Khadijah. Though his elder by 15 years, theirs was a happy and mutually rewarding marriage lasting until her death some 25 years later.

In addition to his exemplary business practices, Muhammad was known for his spiritual sensitivity. Periodically, he would withdraw from the bustle of the city to a place of solitude for periods of meditation and reflection. On one of these sojourns in the year 610, Muhammad had a profound experience, one that would change his life radically—and with it the course of history. While meditating at Mt. Hira near Mecca, he saw a radiant figure on the horizon coming toward him. As the figure, the angel Gabriel, drew near he pronounced the first of the messages that would comprise the Qur'an:

> Recite! In the name of your Lord, who created,
> Created humankind out of a clot.
> Recite! And your Lord is Most Generous,
> He who taught (the use of) the pen,
> Taught humankind what it knew not.
> (Qur'an 96:1–5)

The account of Muhammad's reaction to this experience after his return to Mecca is reminiscent of many of the Hebrew prophets. He was terribly shaken by the encounter and wrestled with the sense of his unworthiness to be God's prophetic messenger. Supported and encouraged by Khadijah and a few close friends, he gradually came to accept his responsibility. By God's choice, not his own, he felt compelled to speak forth the word from the Lord.

Muhammad continued to receive the revelations and proclaim the message for the next twelve years in Mecca. Basic themes in the early revelations included the sublime majesty of the One God, the futility of idol worship, the certainty of God's judgment, and human responsibility for faith in God and fair, compassionate behavior in society. The early converts were few in number, but solid in their conviction. They suffered considerably as subjects of abuse and derision from many Meccans, particularly as the message of the God to whom all were accountable began to threaten the traditional and lucrative polytheistic religious system lodged in Mecca.

In 622, under threat of persecution, Muhammad and seventy companions moved north to Yathrib, later renamed Madina, "the city" (of the prophet). The flight to Yathrib, called the *hijrah*, marks the beginning of the Islamic calendar. In Madina, Muhammad soon achieved prominence as both spiritual and temporal leader. As the Muslim community grew, he challenged and ultimately defeated the powerful Meccan clans. By the time of his death in 632 C.E., Islam had been established in much of Arabia. Within several decades, the new community of faith moved outward with phenomenal success.[3]

Throughout the twenty-three years following the first revelation, Muhammad continued to receive messages. He would recite these and others would both memorize and write down the revelations. The magnificence of the poetic text, uttered by a man known to be unlettered, has always been interpreted by Muslims as a proof of the miraculous process of revelation. Listening to qur'anic recitation leaves little doubt about the lyrical quality and majesty of the text—even if the hearer doesn't know Arabic; but all the more, if he or she does.

In addition to conveying the content of the revelation,

Muhammad also proffered advice and made clear his perspectives on a wide range of subjects. The Qur'an points people of faith to the exemplary life and behavior of Muhammad as a source for guidance in daily life: "Truly, in the messenger of God you have a beautiful model . . ." (Qur'an 33:21). From the outset, faithful Muslims endeavored to preserve accurately the words and deeds of their prophet. Elaborate methods were developed to preserve the authenticity of his words and deeds (*hadith*) through recognized authorities. Collectively, the sayings and actions of Muhammad are called the *sunnah*. Muslims seek to emulate the pattern of behavior presented in the *sunnah* since Muhammad is thought to have lived out the ideals of Islam. While Muslims have always been careful to clarify that Muhammad was a man and in no way to be deified, his particular role has led to special veneration in popular piety.[4]

Early in his distinguished scholarly career as a student of Islam, Wilfred Cantwell Smith articulated the depth of feeling binding Muslims to the prophet:

> Muslims will allow attacks on Allah: there are atheists and atheistic publications, and rationalist societies; but to disparage Muhammad will provoke from even the most "liberal" sections of the community a fanaticism of blazing vehemence.[5]

An awareness of this special love and attachment to Muhammad—a reality, as will be evident in the next chapter, conspicuously missing throughout Western Christendom—helps put the Salman Rushdie episode into some perspective. Without condoning the extremist position calling for Rushdie's death, the depth and breadth of Muslim response is intelligible when viewed in the context of both the Muslim veneration of the prophet and the history of slander against Muhammad emanating from Western sources.

THE QUR'AN

The Qur'an, for Muslims, is the complete, inerrant record of the revelation given through Muhammad. The Qur'an, which literally means "recitation," is understood as having been transmitted in manageable sections over a twenty-three year period. The messages were also perceived as relevant to particular circumstances, known as "the occasions of revelation." When Muslims quote the Qur'an, they affirm, "God says. . . ." As we have noted above, the sayings of the prophet are of great significance for Muslims; they are not, however, to be confused with the Word of God communicated through the Qur'an.

Muhammad is known as the "seal of the prophets," since he is considered the last in a long succession of prophetic messengers through whom God has addressed various human communities. Most of the prophets named in the Qur'an are well-known biblical figures such as Abraham, Moses, David, John the Baptist, and Jesus. The distinction, according to Islam, is that the final revelation through Muhammad, the complete Word of God, has been accurately recorded without error. Thus, the Qur'an and the way of Islam are not considered "new" so much as they are the final and complete guidance for humankind.

Roughly the length of the New Testament, the Qur'an is divided into 114 chapters, called *surahs*. The number of verses, each called an *ayah*, in the chapters varies greatly. With the notable exception of the first *surah*, the Qur'an is generally arranged according to the length of the chapter, with the longest ones first. This arrangement is roughly in reverse of the chronological order in which the messages were proclaimed. Thus, the shortest chapters, found at the end of the Qur'an, were among the first of the Meccan *surahs*; the longer, Madinan chapters are found in the front of the collection. For the person new to the text, this arrangement sometimes creates confusion. Rather than simply pick up the text and begin reading, the student wishing to understand the Qur'an is well-advised to seek assistance.[6]

W. C. Smith offers the following advice for non-Muslims who want to read the Qur'an appreciatively:

> Muslims do not read the Qur'an and conclude that it is divine; rather, they believe it to be divine, then they read it. This makes a great deal of difference, and I urge upon Christian or secular students of the Qur'an that if they wish to understand it as a religious document, they must

approach it in this spirit. If an outsider picks up the book
and goes through it even asking himself, What is there here
that has led Muslims to suppose this from God? he will
miss the reverberating impact. If, on the other hand, he
picks up the book and asks himself, What would these
sentences convey to me if I believed them to be God's
word? then he can much more effectively understand what
has been happening these many centuries in the Muslim
world.[7]

The glorious majesty of God, reflected in the attributes associated with the 99 names of God (e.g., All-Knowing, All-
Powerful, All-Compassionate), is central throughout the Qur'an.
While God is the Transcendent Lord of creation, God is also
intimately connected with human beings. The immanence of
God is portrayed as being closer to humans than their jugular
vein (Qur'an 50:16).

Human responsibility, the certainty of judgment on the Last
Day as well as heaven and hell are vividly proclaimed. The following passage conveys this message as a warning:

> And when the trumpet shall sound a blast,
> And the earth with the mountains shall be lifted up
>   and crushed with one crushing,
> Then, on that day will the Event befall.
> The heavens will split apart, for that day it will be
>   frail,
> And the angels will be on the sides, and on that day
>   eight will bear the throne of their Lord above
>   them.
> On that day you will be exposed; none of your secrets
>   will be hidden.
> Then, as for the one who is given his (record) book
>   in his right hand, he will say: Take, read my book!
> Truly, I knew that I should have to face my reckon-
>   ing.
> Then, he will be in a blissful state
> In a high garden
> Where the clusters are near at hand.

(To those in paradise it will be said): Eat and drink
at ease for that which you sent before you in past
days.

But as for the one who is given his book in his left
hand, he will say, Would that I had not been given
my book

And that I had never known about my reckoning.

Would that death had been my end.

My wealth has not profited me,

My power has gone from me.

(To this one it will be said): Take him and bind him

And then expose him to hell fire,

Then insert him in a chain of seventy cubits length.

Truly, he did not have faith in God, the Tremendous
One,

And was not careful to feed the poor,

Therefore, he has no advocate here this day.

(Qur'an 69: 13-35)

The Qur'an does not present a systematic exposition. It does
include a body of doctrine and practical obligations.[8]

Social and ethical parameters are set in areas such as marriage, divorce, inheritance, responsibility toward children, commercial dealings, food and drink, as well as criminal behavior
such as theft, murder, and adultery. Many of the more detailed
passages prescribing proper behavior are found in the longer
sections revealed during the years in Madina. A section from a
long passage in *surah* 17 illustrates the point.

Your Lord has decreed that you worship none save
Him. Show kindness to your parents. If one or
both of them attain old age with you, do not be
harsh or impatient with them, but speak to them
with kindness.

Lower to them the wing of humility tenderly and say:
My Lord have mercy on them, even as they nurtured me when I was little.

Your Lord knows well what is in your hearts, if you

are righteous. He is all forgiving to those who seek
Him.

Give to the kinsman his due and to the needy and
wayfarer, and do not squander (your wealth) in
wantonness.

Truly, those who squander are brothers to Satan, and
Satan is ever ungrateful before his Lord . . .

Come not near to adultery, which is an abomination
and evil. Do not kill anyone, something God for-
bids except for a righteous cause. If a man is slain
unjustly, We have appointed the next of kin the
right to satisfaction. But let him not carry his ven-
geance beyond what is due, for there is counter
retaliation.

Take care of the property of the orphan with all
integrity, until he comes of age. Keep your covenant, for you are accountable.

Give full measure when you measure, and weigh with
a fair balance. This is better in the end.

Do not pursue things wherein you have no knowledge. Hearing, sight and heart—for each of these
you are held responsible.

Do not strut proudly on the earth. You cannot rend
the earth or match the mountains in stature.

All such behavior is evil in the sight of your Lord.

This is given to you by revelation of the wisdom of
your Lord. Set not any god up beside God lest you
be cast into hell, rebuked and abandoned.

(Qur'an 17:23-27; 32-39)

First and foremost, the Qur'an is meant to be recited, to be
heard and to be experienced. Memorizing and properly reciting
the holy book have been, from the very beginning, important
components in the spiritual life of the faithful. When traveling
in Muslim societies the popularity of Qur'an recitation is immediately obvious by its presence on numerous television and radio
programs as well as at many public gatherings.

THE LIFE OF FAITH AND LIFE IN COMMUNITY

The life of faith begins with the confession, "There is no god, but God, and Muhammad is the messenger of God," called the *shahadah*. Joyful gratitude and obedience to the Creator are manifest in worship and adherence to the requirements established in the Qur'an and secondary sources of authority. The obligatory core components are delineated in five devotional-ritual duties called "the pillars of Islam." The first pillar, the sine qua non, is the *shahadah*.

Prescribed prayer, *salat*, is the second and most conspicuous manifestation of faith. Five times daily, and on special occasions, Muslims are called to prayer from the tall *minarets* in the mosques. Any non-Muslim visiting in a predominantly Muslim country is familiar with the call to prayer echoing throughout the city; most have had the experience of being jolted awake prior to dawn when the first prayer takes place. This common experience fosters a new level of appreciation for the commitment required for such devotional piety. The actual ritual combines several cycles of prayer (primarily recitation of qur'anic passages committed to memory) with different body postures. The worshippers stand in rows of straight lines oriented toward the *Ka'bah*, the central sacred site in Mecca. As with other components of Islamic practice, the unity of the faithful in prayer reflects the conviction that all people stand equally before God.

The third pillar of Islam is almsgiving or religious contribution (*zakat*). Each year, Muslims are expected to contribute approximately 2 1/2% of their overall wealth for the care of the poor and less fortunate. *Zakat* is a religious duty which reflects the conviction that one's resources derive from God and should be used in the service of God. As an institutional form of stewardship, *zakat* is an effective way to support the needs within the community and thereby strengthen the whole.

Each year, Muslims are required to fast (*sawm*) during the daylight hours of the month of Ramadan. Since the Islamic calendar is lunar, the months are continuously moving in relation to the solar calendar. At times, such as the summer in Egypt, the prohibition against eating, drinking, and other normal pleasures from dawn to dusk can be very severe. It is supposed to be a time for self-discipline and serious reflection. Among the benefits, Muslims cite the sense of unity experienced in the fast. Those things that normally divide people — status, class, wealth, race — are removed in the common experience. Moreover, the deprivation increases awareness of the plight of the less fortunate. The entire month is marked by family and community meals after sundown and special meals before sunrise. The month concludes with one of the two major festivals in the Muslim year, a great and joyous celebration to break the fast.

The final pillar is the pilgrimage (*hajj*) at Mecca. At some point in life, Muslims are expected to take part in the pilgrimage during the time set aside for the annual ritual. Unlike the other requirements, the *hajj* is not absolutely obligatory if financial or physical circumstances make the trip impossible. All believers long to take part in the pilgrimage; many literally save money for a lifetime in order to travel to Mecca. Each year, more than two million pilgrims arrive by land, sea, and air to take part in the various rituals spanning several days. Pilgrims don a simple garment made of two white seamless pieces of cloth. Once again, the equality of all people before God is symbolized. The King of Saudi Arabia wears the same garment and worships alongside a person from the lowest caste in India. It matters not. The days of pilgrimage unite Muslims from all over the world even as the rituals link them with sacred events in their history. One has only to talk with a Muslim friend who has taken part in the sacred ceremony to perceive its life-changing impact on the participants.

Woven through these devotional practices are threads uniting Muslims as equal members in the community of faith. Individual responsibility is continuously linked with the well-being of the whole. This community is known as the *ummah*. The *ummah* represented a new and radical departure from social organization in the Arabian clans. At the time of the *hijrah* to Yathrib, the community came clearly into focus as a new entity. It was not accidental that this event, not the birth or death of Muhammad or the first revelation, marked the beginning of the Islamic calendar. The corporate identity within the *ummah* has been a powerful and distinctive characteristic uniting Muslims over the centuries.

This is not to say all has been harmonious within the "house of Islam" (*dar al-islam*). On the contrary, Islamic history is filled with the same types of schism, power struggles, political and military conflicts as one finds in all of human history. The sensitive student of Islamic history will discover a rich religious tradition, inspiring and motivating adherents to their highest good and, at the same time, one replete with fourteen centuries of human foibles.

One of the first major internal controversies surfaced at the time of Muhammad's death. The Muslims were not in agreement concerning the temporal leadership of the community. Some argued that Muhammad had designated Ali, who was both his cousin (the son of Abu Talib) and son-in-law, as his successor. This group was known as the *shi'ah* (the "party" or "faction" supporting Ali; Latinized as Shi'ites). They did not prevail. The majority of Muhammad's closest companions agreed instead on Abu Bakr, one of the first to embrace Islam in Mecca, as the proper successor or *khalifa*. Abu Bakr led the community between 632-34, followed by Umar (634-44) and Uthman (644-56). Finally, after nearly a quarter-century, the internal debate about leadership appeared to be resolved when Ali was selected as the fourth *khalifa* in 656. He ruled for five tumultuous years until his assassination in 661.

With Ali's death, the community was even more deeply divided. The Shi'ites argued for continuing leadership in the family of the prophet through his grandsons (Ali's sons). The larger majority, those who came to be known as the *Sunnis*, the Orthodox, favored instead Mu'awiya. Once again, the Shi'ite views were rejected. These were critical, formative years for the nascent community. The success of rapid growth and expansion also brought forth an array of logistical problems. The internal disagreements festered and erupted into open conflict. In 680, the strong military forces of Mu'awiya's son and successor, Yazid, clashed with a small group of Shi'ites led by Husayn, the grandson of Muhammad. The Shi'ites were annihilated at Karbala, a site in presentday Iraq. From that time forward, Shi'ites have commemorated the martyrdom of the faithful and incorporated redemptive suffering into the theological perspectives informing the various groupings among them.

What began as a question of succession developed over the centuries into substantial differences in theology and worldview between Sunnis and Shi'ites. Within each of the two large branches various schools developed around theological and philosophical and legal interpretation. The study of the intellectual developments within Islam reveals how rich and diverse are the components that comprise the mosaic. Overall, the Sunnis account for approximately 80–85% and the Shi'ites 15–20% of the total Muslim population today. Aside from a few exceptions, Shi'ite leaders have generally not controlled temporal power. The rise to power of Shi'ite religious leaders through the 1979 revolution in Iran, a country whose populace is over 90% Shi'ite, is one of those exceptions.

For all Muslims, the divinely ordered pattern of human conduct within the *ummah* is set forth in the *shari'ah* ("the way," the right path for ritual and ethical action). The *shari'ah* is the collective body of teaching based on the Qur'an and the *sunnah* of the prophet. It includes binding laws clarifying how the faithful should conduct themselves in relation to God and in all manner of human relationships. The processes employed to develop this body of law are many and complex. They include legal scholars working within different schools of jurisprudence as well as the collective wisdom or consensus of the *ummah* established over the centuries. Even now, the debate continues within Islam as to whether the process of refining and elaborating on the *shari'ah* is valid.

Early in Islamic history another "way," another spiritual path, developed alongside and intertwined with the Sunni and Shi'ite sectarian schools of thought: the "way" of the mystics. Extremely popular and far-reaching in their influence, the mystics (*sufis*) of Islam have been a consistent presence in all parts of the Muslim world. Rooted in the teachings in the Qur'an, *sufi* leaders and groups struck a popular chord among many of the faithful despite the formidable opposition, even persecution, from orthodox religious leadership. In their various manifestations, the *sufis* have both complicated and enriched the *ummah* for more than a millennium.[9] Their popular appeal, particularly in central and southern Asia where there was already a long tradition of mystical religiosity, accounts, in part, for the pervasive spread of Islam.

THE SPREAD AND INFLUENCE OF ISLAMIC CIVILIZATION

During its first century, missionary zeal and military prowess extended Islamic influence from Spain to India. After this initial outward thrust, Islam continued to spread through the persuasive power of its message, often carried by merchants, and its vibrant, thriving civilization. The Western image of Islam as inherently backward, anti-intellectual and unsophisticated quickly disappears in the face of even a cursory survey of Islamic history. The error of the image is particularly ironic in view of the major contributions and influences that helped shape Western civilization as we know it. Indigenous Arab Christians and Christian converts to Islam were also very much a part of this process, but the dominant impetus came from within Islam.

A sampling of English words originating within Muslim cultures provides a clue to the primary areas of influence: admiral, alchemy, alcohol, alcove, alfalfa, algebra, arsenal, assassin, average, balcony, cable, candy, checkmate, coffee, cotton, divan, elixir, frieze, gala, giraffe, guitar, jasmine, lemon, lute, magazine, mask, mat, nadir, orange, rice, sapphire, sofa, sugar, syrup, tariff, zenith, zero. Western civilization incorporated the advanced accomplishments of the Muslims in science, engineering, navigation, mathematics, medicine, astronomy, philosophy, architecture, calligraphy and horticulture. Examples in three areas—philosophy, mathematics, and horticulture—illustrate the degree of indebtedness.

In the 8th century, Arab scholars returned from India with a system of numbers. By adding the zero, Arab mathematicians created a system capable of solving complicated problems. By the 9th century, scholars had developed algebra; later generations of Muslim scientists explored geometry and trigonometry. Sophisticated mathematical developments led to pioneering work in astronomy as well. For Muslims, theological and devotional concerns were related to these scholarly pursuits. In algebra, for example, they employed symbols indicating infinite possibilities. This concept mirrors the theological conviction of God's limitless nature and unbounded work in creation. Practical benefits of mathematical advances included precision in developing calendars and the ability to orient people accurately toward Mecca for daily worship. By the 13th century, the Arabic numerals (the name still used for our numbers) had replaced the old Roman numerals. The knowledge and advances by Muslim scholars were foundational to the subsequent scientific development in the West.

A famous *hadith* widely attributed to Muhammad urges Muslims to "seek knowledge wherever it can be found, even unto China." Motivated by this injunction, Muslims explored the classical Greek texts lying dormant in Byzantine libraries. Working from Greek through Syriac into Arabic, scholars, assisted at times by Arab Christians, translated numerous classical texts in order to appropriate the insights into their search for a rational exposition of the faith. Over several centuries, these translations and the brilliant writings of Muslim thinkers such as al-Kindi, al-Farabi, Ibn Sina (Avicenna) and Ibn Rushd (Averroes), the Greek philosophical and metaphysical tradition was reintroduced to Europe. Translations of their writings from Arabic into Latin were instrumental in the formative work of European scholars like St. Thomas Aquinas and Roger Bacon.

The culinary tradition in Europe and the Americas derived a great deal through interaction with the peoples of Islam. Both in their role as conduits and resourceful cultivators of the land, Muslims contributed greatly in the area of horticulture. From their contacts in India, for example, Muslims introduced the orange tree and sugarcane into the western provinces (including Spain). Other foods and spices such as rice, melons, dates, lemons, pepper, ginger, and cloves came West through contact with the Muslims. Moreover, Muslims in Spain introduced the cultivation of cotton, advanced new techniques for irrigation, methods of grafting, soil conditioning, and curative treatments for diseased trees. If all of this is not enough to merit appreciation, the next time you enjoy a hot cup of coffee, remember that it was the Arabs who provided this elixir of life to the rest of the world via the spread of Islamic civilization.

ISLAM IN THE WORLD TODAY

Following centuries of unprecedented growth and development, the extensive Islamic empire entered a long period of uneven decline. Various political and military developments altered the map in Asia and the Mediterranean region. Some portions of the Islamic world continued to flourish while other areas were subjugated to non-Muslim rule. From the 16th to the 20th centuries, most of the predominantly Muslim lands were under the control of outside political powers. This heritage of domination — particularly by the Ottoman Turks and European colonial powers — is a key factor influencing the behavior of many Muslims advocating change today.

The Islamic revival movement surged into popular consciousness in the West with the Iranian revolution. In fact, various elements of the reform and renewal had been developing during the past two centuries. It is a multifaceted phenomenon with emphases differing from country to country. John Esposito, a well-known student of contemporary Islam, summarized current developments with these observations:

> Islamic revivalism in its broadest sense refers to a renewal of Islam in Muslim personal and public life. Its manifestations include an increase in religious observances (mosque attendance, Ramadan fast, wearing traditional Islamic dress); a revitalization of sufi (mystical) orders; proliferation of religious publications and media programming; calls for the implementation of Islamic law; creation of Islamic banks; and the growth of Islamic organizations and activist movements.
>
> Growing out of this context, Islamic revivalism has led to the reassertion of Islam in politics. Incumbent governments appeal to Islam for political legitimacy and popular support for policies and programs. Opposition movements use the language and symbols of Islam to criticize established governments, and to advocate actions ranging from socio-political reform to violent revolutionary action.

The forms that Islamic revivalism takes vary almost infi-
nitely from one country to another, but there are certain
themes: a sense that existing political, economic, and social
systems have failed; a disenchantment with and even rejection of the West; a quest for identity and greater authenticity; and the conviction that Islam provides a self-
sufficient ideology for state and society, a valid alternative
to secular nationalism, socialism, and capitalism.[10]

Esposito accurately identifies common themes and concerns
while, at the same time, underscoring the diversity found in
different countries. Any effort to understand the dynamics
related to upheaval or the demand for change must take seriously the particular context. Sweeping generalizations inevitably
lead to erroneous conclusions. Even though Great Britain, Swe-
den, and Italy are all Western European countries with predominantly Christian populations, no serious person wanting to
understand developments in these countries would draw quick
generalizations and assume they fit in all three contexts. Similarly, Lebanon, Egypt, Iran, and Pakistan represent four very
distinct settings, each requiring analysis on its own terms.

In many areas of turbulence today it is possible to identify
problems related to the lingering colonial legacy. Frequently,
the boundaries of nation-states divide people arbitrarily. What
sense does it make to divide the Kurds into four different countries (Iran, Turkey, Syria and Iraq)? or the Soviet and Iranian
Azerbaijanis into two? An even more common source of
national frustration stems from unrepresentative government
leadership. At the beginning of the 1990s, many countries where
Muslims comprise the majority are ruled by a monarchy or military government. Rarely are such leaders in power by virtue of
popular choice. Frequently, the relationships binding such countries to regional and global powers keep them in a position of
dependency. Add in the all too familiar pattern of corruption
and excess and you have a recipe for popular discontent. A
leader like the ex-Shah of Iran, for instance, was quite at home
with the wealthy "jet set" in Europe and Western government
leaders; he had little to do with the orientation and aspirations
of the vast majority of Iranians.

Muslims are not alone in the movement to remove unrepresentative and oppressive governments. They are distinctive, however, in that traditional Islamic structures and an inclusive worldview have proven effective for organizing opposition and developing alternatives to the status quo. But even when dramatic change occurs, as in the Iranian revolution, the picture remains complex. While the Iranians consciously endeavored to institute an "Islamic Republic," for instance, they drew heavily on structures of parliamentary democracies in Western Europe. The Iranians declared a "republic," a modern, non-Islamic notion; they adopted a constitution; their *majlis* (Parliament) is elected by popular vote; the government is structured with a Ministry of Justice, a Foreign Ministry, and so forth. Thus, even in an explicit effort to structure an Islamic state, the experiment blends modern political constructs with Shi'ite interpretation of traditional Islamic governmental structures.

These observations underscore why Esposito and other observers of contemporary Islam insist on contextual analysis rooted in an accurate understanding of the religious tradition and political history. This type of approach is rather far removed, unfortunately, from the simplistic, stereotypical images served up in the popular media. These images are particularly powerful both because of the influence of the television and because they often connect with and reinforce the long-standing bias against Arabs, Muslims and Islam. In the first chapter we indentified the pervasiveness of this Western prejudice. We urged refraining from judgment and empathetic understanding as useful means to develop a new, more accurate knowledge of Islam.

It is not enough, however, to refrain temporarily from judgment. We must endeavor to comprehend what has brought Christians and Muslims to this point in their history of interaction. The value of an historical overview goes beyond setting the context for present attitudes and perspectives. The process has the added benefit of helping to clarify the issues around which Christians and Muslims have disagreed—or assumed that they were in disagreement. In the next chapter, therefore, we turn attention to a survey of Christian views of Islam and an examination of the primary elements informing Islamic understanding of Christianity. The stage will then be set to look forward to the future and ask: Are there other options for future interfaith relationships? What is required to chart a new course for adherents in the world's two largest religious traditions?

CHAPTER THREE

The History of Christian-Muslim Relations: An Overview

The history of Christian-Muslim encounter is as old as Islam. Rooted in the monotheistic tradition of the patriarch Abraham, Christians and Muslims share a common heritage. For more than fourteen centuries, adherents of these two communities of faith have travelled a long and often difficult road together. There have been some bright spots along the way. In addition to periods of great tension, hostility, and open conflict, one can discover considerable positive interaction. At points, the relationship has extended beyond uneasy toleration to peaceful coexistence. On balance, however, the history of the interaction has been characterized by mistrust, misunderstanding and mutual antipathy. Why have these two communities clashed so vigorously through the centuries? What informs the sense of mistrust that pervades the history of Christian-Muslim relations and skews attempts to relate more constructively today?

Religious diversity always poses a challenge to the self-understanding of religious communities. Early church history reveals the internal debates among Christians concerning the proper understanding and relationship with Jews and others in the Mediterranean world. In the second century, Christian thinkers often drew sharp distinctions between pagan religious practices and the way of Christ. At the same time, influential Christians such as Justin Martyr and Clement of Alexandria discovered much in Greek philosophical thought that complemented Christian theological understanding.[1]

The conversion of Constantine and the establishment of Christianity as the state religion in the fourth century served to shift Christian attitudes toward other religious movements into the realm of public policy. The very community which had sought tolerance from the Roman government and distinction from pagan practices often became intolerant of those who did not embrace Christianity and those who were regarded as heretics.

CHRISTIAN UNDERSTANDING OF ISLAM PRIOR TO THE 19TH CENTURY

The advent of Islam in the seventh century presented Christians with new issues and problems. In the short space of a century, Islam transformed the character and culture of many lands from India to Spain, disrupted the unity of the Mediterranean world and displaced the axis of Christendom to the north. Contrary to popular opinion, the Muslims did not come out of the Arabian desert plundering everything in sight and forcing conversions at the point of a sword.[2] Rather, the expansion of Islamic rule was a multifaceted phenomenon. The Arab conquest was facilitated by the religious and political situation in Syria, Palestine, and Egypt. The Syriac-and Coptic-speaking Orthodox churches were decidedly anti-Greek in sentiment. Their strong rejection of the Chalcedonian orthodoxy the emperors had endeavored to impose encouraged a subdued response to Islam, at times even welcoming the Muslims rather than resisting them.[3]

Nevertheless, the swift conquest of Egypt, Palestine, and Syria greatly impressed the Byzantines and caused them to ponder its significance. Unfortunately, we possess only scattered fragments from the pens of seventh-century Christians on the subject. These materials provide insight into intra-Christian conflicts and rivalries; they do not critique Islam as such.[4] There is no known Byzantine tract of that century devoted specifically to the problem of Islam and/or the Arab conquest. The first coherent treatment of the subject is found in the writing of John of

Damascus (died ca. 750 C.E.). John was reared in Damascus in close proximity to the administrative and military center of Islam during the Umayyad dynasty (661–750). His firsthand acquaintance with Islam led him to treat it not as an alien tradition, but as a Christian heresy. Viewed positively, this indicates that John found much in the Qur'an and the Muslim community that was compatible with the gospel.[5] His writings mark the beginning of a long and often bitter, polemical exchange between the adherents of these two religious traditions.

Islam challenged Christian assumptions. Not only was Islam an obvious worldly success, it also presented a puzzling and threatening new intellectual position. A sizeable portion of the Christian community was absorbed into Islam in the decades following the advent of Islamic rule. With the notable exception of the Coptic Orthodox Church in Egypt, the once thriving Christian communities across North Africa virtually disappeared after the seventh century. Since forced conversion was not the primary reason for the phenomenon, the power of Islamic theology and ideology cannot be ignored. R. W. Southern frames the issues succinctly:

> To acknowledge one God, an omnipotent creator of the universe, but to deny the Trinity, the Incarnation, and the divinity of Christ was an intelligible philosophical position made familiar by many ancient thinkers. Likewise, to profess the immortality of the soul, the existence of a future state of rewards and punishments, and the need for such good works as almsgiving as a requirement for entry into Paradise was recognizable in this same context. But what was to be made of a doctrine that denied the divinity of Christ and the fact of his crucifixion, but acknowledged his virgin birth and his special privileges as a prophet of God; that treated the Old and New Testaments as the Word of God, but gave sole authority to a volume which intermingled confusingly the teachings of both testaments; that accepted the philosophically respectable doctrine of future rewards and punishments, but affronted philosophy by suggesting that sexual enjoyment would form the chief delight in Paradise?[6]

Not all medieval Christian thinkers could have articulated major distinctions between Christianity and Islam with such clarity. Still, most of these ideas were circulating in some form. Christians may have been misinformed, but they were rarely completely uninformed or neutral with respect to Islam. Almost all Christian interpreters spoke in terms of its deficiencies. At best, Islam was considered a Christian heresy. More often, however, malicious and absurd distortions about the tenets of Islam and the character of Muhammad characterized the perception of Christians. This was particularly true in Europe following the low point in Christian-Muslim relations: the Crusades.

The Crusades were launched at the end of the eleventh century (1096 C.E.), ostensibly to recapture the Holy Land from the Muslims. In fact, several factors weighed heavily in the religious and political machinations that compelled European Christians to mount eight crusades over the following two centuries. Beyond the religious zeal to reclaim the holy sites, the tensions between Eastern and Western Christendom in the aftermath of the great schism of 1054 played a significant role. The measure of internal Christian animosity is reflected in the suffering experienced by Eastern Orthodox Christians — not to mention Jewish communities — during the various onslaughts. The search for new trade routes to the East was yet another factor encouraging the massive military expeditions.

Although the Crusades are no longer viewed as noble or exemplary of responsible Christian behavior, they did cast a long shadow for many centuries. Medieval writers were inspired by the stories of chivalry and fighting for holy causes. Not surprisingly, the picture of Islam that permeated Europe was decidedly unfavorable. Norman Daniel has produced the most thorough study of Islam in the eyes of Latin Christians. His work, which focuses on the 12th through the 14th centuries, documents the almost universally negative images of Islam in the West.[7]

Many Europeans perceived Islam as a product of the Devil or Antichrist, something to be opposed and fought at every turn. The prophet's followers, it was alleged, worshipped him as a god. One explanation for the origin of Islam was that Muhammad was a cardinal who failed to get elected pope and, in revenge, seceded from the church. It was commonly believed that Muhammad had trained a dove to sit on his shoulder as a prop to deceive followers into thinking that he spoke as one inspired by God. Another exceedingly degrading and widespread story reported that Muhammad had been killed by swine while in the process of urinating. The list goes on and on. The prevailing sentiment is captured in the picture of a mutilated Muhammad languishing in the depths of hell in Dante's *Inferno*:

> No cask without an end stave or a head
> E'er gaped so wide as one shade I beheld,
> Cloven from chin to where the wind is voided.
> Between his legs his entrails hung in coils;
> The vitals were exposed to view, and too
> That sorry paunch which changes food to filth.
> While I stood all absorbed in watching him
> He looked at me and stretched his breast apart,
> Saying, "Behold, how I split myself!
> In front of me the weeping Ali goes,
> His face cleft through from forelock to chin;
> And all the others you see about
> Fomentors were of discord and of schism:
> And that is why they are so gashed asunder."[8]

There were, happily, a few inquisitive and courageous church leaders who sought to understand Islam correctly, albeit for purposes of refutation. In the middle of the 12th century, the Qur'an was translated into Latin under the direction of Peter the Venerable. Peter justified the project, which was strongly criticized by Bernard of Clairvaux among others, on the grounds that Islam was a Christian heresy and must be understood on its own terms before it could be answered.[9]

Francis of Assisi, in the midst of the Crusades, visited the Sultan of Egypt. Impressed by the Muslim call to prayer, St. Francis encouraged the friars to announce worship services with church bells. In his instructions to brothers who were going to live in Muslim lands, Francis emphasized that they were to live among the Muslims in peace, avoiding quarrels and disputes.[10] In recognition of this openness to others and his commitment to peace, Pope John Paul II invited many religious leaders from all traditions to gather in Assisi on October 26, 1986, for a day of prayer for world peace.

In the middle of the 15th century there came what Southern calls "a moment of vision"[11] during which the notion of dialogue between people of faith was put forward. The most positive spirit of this brief era is exemplified in the writings of Nicholas of Cusa; the idea is found also in the writings of John of Segovia, Jean Germain, and Aeneas Silvius.

Nicholas (1401-64) was a Renaissance man. He immersed himself in political, ecclesiastical, and intellectual affairs through travel and reading. His *De Pace Fidei* (Concerning the Harmony of the Faiths) is an imaginary dialogue between members of different religious traditions. Set in a kind of heavenly council with seventeen participants, the dialogue reveals a fundamental unity in religion even though each community worships God by different rites and under different names. The Word of God chairs the heavenly council. The Word, not the sword, represents the most powerful response to religious diversity.[12]

Nicholas' later work, *Cribratio Alchorani* (Sifting of the Qur'an), written at the request of the pope, attempts to distinguish the Christian and non-Christian elements in the Qur'an in order to refute the errors of Islam. On balance, Nicholas offers a positive view of human religiosity. His efforts to deal constructively with the problem of religious pluralism in general and Islam and the Qur'an in particular, reveal both his commitment to accuracy and his creativity.

The spirit exemplified by Nicholas of Cusa was shortlived. Martin Luther's writings less than a century later convey the more prevalent sentiment: deep animosity towards Islam. Like most other leaders during the ages of the definitive Western schism, Luther was not preoccupied with the significance of non-Christian religions in his writings. The issue arose primarily in connection with the threat posed by the Ottoman Turks. Consequently, much of what Luther wrote on the subject was linked directly to the political and military realities of his time.

From the fall of Constantinople onwards, Christians in Europe were terror-stricken. By 1526, the armies of Sulaiman II had conquered Hungary and were literally at the Austrian border. For Luther and his contemporaries, the threat of Ottoman hegemony was very real. In one of the ironies of history, this impending danger actually served as a protection for Luther.

> The empire needed the help of the evangelical princes in the war against the Turks and therefore had to postpone its plans to destroy Luther. From the point of view of realistic power politics, the safety of the Reformation depended on the strength of the Turkish army.[13]

Whatever the political dynamics, Luther's views on Islam were unambiguous. In his *Von Krieg wider den Turken* (On War Against the Turks), Luther calls the Turks' god "the devil" and Turks "the servants of the devil." He states his desire to obtain a whole copy of the Qur'an (he already had pieces of it) so he could translate it into German for everyone to see "what a foul and shameful book it is." He provides this analysis of the Qur'an:

> He (Muhammad) greatly praises Christ and Mary as being the only ones without sin, and yet he believes nothing more of Christ than that he is a holy prophet, like Jeremiah or Jonah and denies that He is God's Son and true God. . . . On the other hand, Mohammed highly exalts and praises himself and boasts that he has talked with God and the angels. . . . From this anyone can easily see that Mohammed is a destroyer of our Lord Christ and his kingdom. . . . Father, Son, Holy Ghost, baptism, the sacrament, gospel, faith, and all Christian doctrine are gone, and instead of Christ only Mohammed and his doctrine of works and especially of the sword is left.[14]

Luther and Dante are representative of the prevailing views among European Christians. While there were alternative voices offering a somewhat more positive perspective, these were far less audible at the time and less influential in subsequent thinking. Islam is the only major religious tradition and civilization that ever threatened Christianity once it spread out from Palestine. The deep sense of fear and hostility toward Islam is palpable, not only in the writings of Dante and Luther, but throughout Western literature. This bias, rooted in inaccurate and invidious caricature, is a firm fixture in the cultural heritage bequeathed to contemporary Western civilization.

Several developments in the 19th and 20th centuries began to challenge conventional views, at least among scholars and a segment of Christian leaders in Europe and North America. Before considering those developments, we turn first to an overview of Islamic understanding of Christianity.

MUSLIM VIEWS ON CHRISTIANITY

Awareness of and discussions about the biblical tradition are woven into Islamic self-understanding. Just as the early Christians struggled to identify the proper understanding of and relationship with the Jewish community, so Muslims were challenged vis-à-vis both Christians and Jews. Muhammad and his companions were guided by the Qur'an which they understood as a continuation and completion of God's revelations to humankind. This self-conscious awareness provided Muslims a significantly different point of departure. The Qur'an enjoined the "people of the Book" (*ahl al-kitab*) to align with Muslims in affirming the central truth about the One God:

> O people of the Book, come to a common word between us and you, that we worship none but God, and that we associate nothing with Him, and that none of us take others for lords apart from God. (Qur'an 3:64)

Since most Jews and Christians failed to embrace Islam in the manner here envisioned, the relationships developed with far less amity and far more complexity than the early Muslims had hoped.

The Qur'an presents a very positive view of Jesus. He is mentioned by name in 93 different verses scattered in 15 chapters. He is called a prophet, a messenger, a servant of God, a Word from God, the Messiah and one inspired or aided by the Spirit of God. These latter three are particularly intriguing as distinctive titles among the prophetic figures in the Qur'an. The designation "Word" is linked primarily to Jesus' uniqueness in birth. The Qur'an identifies Jesus with Adam:

> The angels said: O Mary! Behold, God
>   brings you good news of a word from Him, whose name
>   is the Messiah, Jesus, son of Mary . . .
> She said: My Lord! How can I have a child when no human
>   has touched me? He said: It will be so. God creates
>   what He wills. If He declares something, He need only
>   say: Be! and it is . . .
> Behold! The likeness of Jesus with God is the likeness of
>   Adam. He created him out of dust, then said to him:
>   Be! and he is. (Qur'an 3:45, 47, 49)

On eleven occasions, the Qur'an speaks of Jesus as the Messiah; in seven verses, the "Spirit of God" is directly associated with Jesus. The precise meaning of these titles is not clearly explained. In one passage both terms are used as the unity of God is emphasized for those in danger of going astray. This text specifically addresses fundamental Christian tenets:

> O People of the Book, do not exceed beyond the bounds
> in your religion or say things about God, save the truth.
> The Messiah, Jesus, son of Mary, is only a messenger of
> God, and His word which He conveyed to Mary, and a
> spirit from Him. So believe in God and His messengers,
> and say not, "Three." Stop. It is better for you. God is
> only one God. It is far removed from His majesty that He
> should have a son. (Qur'an 4:171)

Jesus is exalted in the Qur'an as one of the greatest, even unique, among God's prophets. The points of conflict, according to the Qur'an, arise in relation to the erroneous teachings propagated by Christians. In fact, the Qur'an contains both a harsh critique of and kind words for the followers of Jesus. At times, Christians are chided for having distorted the revelation of God. They are called *kuffar* ("those who reject or say 'no' to God; infidels"), people whose doctrines flirt with the most heinous of all sins, *shirk* ("associating something with God"). Numerous passages warn against people whose dangerous doctrines are an affront to God. Most notably, the divinity of Christ and the doctrine of the Trinity are rejected. Both are seen as compromising the unity and transcendence of God.

But this is not the whole picture. The Qur'an leaves no doubt about the salvific value of at least some religious traditions:

> Behold! Those who have faith, and those who are Jews, Christians and Sabaeans[15]—those who trust in God and the Last Day, and do what is righteous, they shall have their reward; no fear shall come upon them, neither shall they grieve. (Qur'an 2:62 and 5:69)

Grave warnings against doctrinal error notwithstanding, the Qur'an sets forth clear principles to guide Muslims in their relationships with Christians (and other communities of faith). The different religious communities should exist in complete freedom. The famous qur'anic declaration asserts: "There shall be no compulsion in religious matters" (Qur'an 2:256).

The different religious communities are explained as part of God's plan. The diversity is caused, ironically, by different reactions to the various prophets, despite their having been given revelation from the same source. If God had so willed, the Qur'an declares, humankind would be one community. The fact that humankind is divided into various communities is explained as a test for people of faith. The emphasis falls on responsible behavior here in this life.

> If God had so willed, He would have made all of you one community, but (He has not done so) that He may test you in what He has given you; so compete with one another in good works. To God you shall all return and He will tell you (the truth) about that which you have been disputing. (Qur'an 5:48)

As with all human history and experience, there exists a gap between the principles and ideals in a religious tradition—as articulated by a founder, its sacred text(s) or the wisdom of tradition—and the practice of the adherents through the years.

For Muslims, the positive principles in the Qur'an have been less evident in relation to Christian communities through the centuries than have disputes and accusations arising from theological differences. With few exceptions, most Islamic literature on Christianity has been framed in the language of polemics.[16] Recurring themes include charges of altering or forging parts of the divine revelation, seriously errant doctrine (e.g., original sin, incarnation, atonement, the Trinity) and grievous mistakes in religious practice (e.g., celibacy, veneration of saints, "idol" worship).

As we have seen with Christian interpretations of Islam, Muslim positions were developed often on partial, inadequate, superficial, or erroneous information about the wider Christian tradition. Understanding and articulating the human/divine nature of Christ and the Oneness of God manifest in the Trinity were the very issues that divided Christians in the earliest ecumenical councils. For Muslim critics, however, the subtleties of these issues were largely unknown or irrelevant. Further, Muslim writers, like their Christian counterparts, did not work in a vacuum. Inevitably, changing political and military exigencies played a substantial role in the thinking and priorities of individual writers as well as religious and political leaders.

Having noted the similar dynamics at work among Muslim and Christian writers, it is important to stress one major difference between the predominant orientation in the respective approaches. Most Christian interpreters in the West began with the assumption that Islam was, by definition, false. The finality of God's redemptive action in Jesus Christ was the definitive event for human history. A new religion arising after Christianity, the reasoning goes, must be false or a heretical deviation from the faith. The worldly success of Islam and the threat it posed to Christendom deepened the anxiety and confirmed the predisposition that Islam was dangerous and evil. Hence the easy connection and popular acceptance that Muhammad was somehow linked to the Devil or Antichrist.

Muslims, on the other hand, began with the assumption that Jesus was one of the greatest among the special messengers from God. They assumed that the revelation he brought was true and accurate. The frustration and fear vis-à-vis Christendom was never vented through fraudulent or derogatory assaults on Jesus. Rather, it is the distortions and even blasphemous teachings and practices of the Christian community that Muslims feel need to be addressed. The foundation for Christians, and for that matter Jews and other communities of faith, is legitimate. The truth that should guide them, however, has been obscured. Why Christians cannot see this and see with clarity the truth of God's revelation in the Qur'an has always puzzled most Muslims. So long as they do not embrace Islam, Christians living under Islamic rule are to be treated as "protected peoples" (*dhimmis*). The practical implications of *dhimmi* status fluctuated from time to time and place to place. But the principle remains: Christianity rests on the true revelation of God through Jesus, and Christians, however much they have distorted the revelation, are a legitimate community deserving "protection" under Islamic authority.

These different orientations, rooted in the fundamental tenets of both traditions, cannot be passed over lightly. For many people in both communities the basic theological issues constitute the primary agenda for Christian-Muslim dialogue. Understanding different orientations is an important step, but it does not resolve the seemingly inherent conflicts. Thoughtful, creative, and persevering efforts are required in order to bridge some of the real and perceived differences in foundational theological understandings.

After more than a millenium of confrontation and interaction, the operative dynamics began to change in the 19th century. Although we all carry the cumulative baggage provided by our deep-rooted heritage, developments in the past 150 years have challenged traditional assumptions and prompted the vexing questions confronting people of faith today.

DEVELOPMENTS IN THE 19TH AND 20TH CENTURIES

Changes in Western Christian attitudes and patterns of relationship with Muslims during the past century have occurred in the context of the larger interreligious encounter. Three major developments have been crucial to the process.

First, constantly improving means of transportation and communication have facilitated international commerce and unprecedented levels of migration among all people. The awareness of religious pluralism and global interdependence has grown steadily. In recent years, as we noted in the first chapter, the impact of these issues is being felt even at the local level throughout the West.

Second, the rise in the academic study of comparative religion stimulated scholars to amass a wealth of information on the world's various religious practices and belief systems.[17] Beginning in the 19th century, the self-consciously scientific approach to the study of religious traditions revealed how biased and uninformed were many of the views held by Western Christians over the centuries. Although we now take the study of religion for granted, the 19th century initiative marked a dramatic turning point in religious understanding. Religious insights and behavior were no longer relegated only to piety and practice. In addition to feeling or believing something, the new component of critical reflection became part of the mix. The process led to new perceptions, new ways of seeing human religiosity.

A manifestation of this shift in Western perception occurred in 1840 when Thomas Carlyle included a lecture on Muhammad ("The Hero as Prophet") in his famous series on *Heroes and Hero Worship*. Carlyle's reading of the Qur'an and consideration of Islam led him to conclude that Muhammad was sincere and devout. While his overall analysis is woefully inadequate by today's standards of scholarship, Carlyle succeeded in challenging the prevailing view of Muhammad as a shrewd and sinister charlatan. Subsequently, scholars were obliged to reflect on their presuppositions and sources of authority in more objective terms.

Third, another 19th century development in the West, the modern missionary movement, occasioned a new, more sophisticated awareness of Muslims as well as other people of faith. Although the motivating impetus, the orientation, and ultimate goals often have been quite dissimilar, there have been points at which Western scholars and missionaries converged in their respective efforts to understand other religious traditions. The line is not always easy to discern since some prominent academicians—theologians, historians and phenomenologists of religion—have themselves served as missionaries.

The importance of personal contact and conversation with adherents of other traditions figured significantly in both the scholarly and missionary endeavors. In the initial stage, scholars gathered, recorded, studied, and interpreted data from the religious traditions; the second stage included human encounter: the people being studied were present. In 1959, W.C. Smith summarized the trends in scholarly circles and looked forward to the next phases.

> The traditional form of Western scholarship in the study of other men's religion was that of an impersonal presentation of an "it." The first great innovation in recent times has been the personalization of the faiths observed, so that one finds a discussion of a "they." Presently the observer becomes personally involved, so that the situation is one of a "we" talking about a "they." The next step is a dialogue, where "we" talk to "you." If there is listening and mutuality, this may become that "we" talk *with* "you." The culmination of the process is when "we all" are talking *with* each other about "us."[18]

Later in the same article, Smith linked the academic trend with developments in the churches.

> To talk about people is not the same as to talk to them; nor is it quite the same as to talk with them. The need for these last two steps in comparative religion is beginning to be felt only gradually perhaps in universities but urgently by the churches. The word "dialogue" has actually been coming much to the fore in recent years, with both the Roman Catholic Church and the Protestant. Major movements are afoot.[19]

Another prominent 20th-century historian of religion, Fredrich Heiler, believed that the knowledge derived through interreligious encounter would itself play a significant role in the future of the world's religious traditions. His experience revealed that the study of the history of religion conveys "the wondrous wealth of religions," creates a sense of "esteem for other religions," provides insight into the falsity of numerous polemical judgments of past times, and reveals "the close relationship existing among outwardly differing religions." He fervently hoped that the scientific study of religion would assist in preparing the way for "a new era . . . when the religions will rise to true tolerance and co-operation" in behalf of humanity.[20]

This hope for a new era of cooperation is found among missionary agencies and personnel in this century. The concern surfaces explicitly in the respective dialogue programs launched after 1960 by the Vatican and the World Council of Churches. It represents one component of the "major movements afoot" in the 20th century, to which we will turn our attention in chapter five. Such contemporary developments reflect responses to issues arising during the last century.

In 1893, the World Parliament of Religions was convened in Evanston, Illinois. The gathering was designed as an ecumenical Christian meeting to rethink the presuppositions of Christian exclusivity. Although the Parliament included only a handful of representatives from non-Christian traditions, they were articulate and engaging. The notables included Swami Vivekananda, founder of the Vedanta Society of America, and Dharmapala, the Ceylonese founder of the Young Men's Buddhist Association. Their presence and active participation was a powerful statement on the value of inclusiveness even in the process of clarifying self-understanding. American Muslims also were in attendance. Alexander Russell (Mohammed) Webb, a former American diplomat and a convert, was the major defender of Islam. George Washburn, an American missionary who served as president of Robert College in Constantinople, offered an extended, point-by-point scholarly comparison of Islam and Christianity.

As more accurate knowledge of Islam, the Hindu tradition, religious traditions in Japan, and so forth, increased in the West, traditional Christian theological assumptions and exclusivist claims began to be reassessed. The central issues discussed in the three great missionary conferences of the early 20th century reflect this internal debate. Further, they serve as a prelude to the interreligious dialogue movement.

At the time of the First World Missionary Conference, which was held in Edinburgh in 1910, few missiologists were outwardly questioning the foundational premise of *extra ecclesiam nulla salus* (there is no salvation outside the church). Rather, the focus was on a strategic review of the world as a mission field for Western Christians, and Protestants in particular.

When the Second World Missionary Conference convened eighteen years later in Jerusalem, the mood was considerably different. Hendrick Kraemer, a Dutch scholar and church leader, offered these insights on the difference in the first two World Missionary Conferences:

> The Jerusalem meeting in 1928 moves in quite a different atmosphere ... the mood is more introspective and observant than strategical. Faith and natural Western self-confidence have been more differentiated by the purifying fire of reality and experience. The unequivocal disavowal at Jerusalem of all spiritual imperialism is one of the clearest symptoms of this change.[21]

After nearly a century of intense Western missionary activity, the fervor was beginning to wane in some quarters. The "disavowal of all spiritual imperialism" reflected the growing conviction that a proper missionary response of the West toward the new awakenings in the East was not found primarily in conversions, but in Christian service. The ambiguity related to responsible and faithful Christian mission clearly surfaced in Jerusalem.

Two years after the Jerusalem meeting, a group of lay-Christians organized a commission to reassess the mission enterprise. The commission, chaired by William E. Hocking, the Harvard philosopher of religion, produced a substantial report which affirmed the continuation of Christian mission, but stressed the necessity of a genuine effort to understand and appreciate other religious traditions. The inquiry underscored the importance of tolerance on moral and theological grounds.

> It is clearly not the duty of the Christian missionary to attack other faiths ... the Christian will regard himself as

a co-worker with the forces within each religious system which are making for righteousness.[22]

The stage was now set for the Third World Missionary Conference. Hendrik Kraemer was asked to prepare a document prior to the 1938 conference in Tambaram (near Madras). The result was his book, *The Christian Message in a Non-Christian World*. On the key issue of how Christians should understand and relate to adherents of other religious traditions, Kraemer set forth an approach which held firmly that God "expressed clearly and exclusively in Christ's life and work His judgment on, and purpose for man and the world." The evangelistic posture he espoused, however, required the proclamation of the message of God "in a persuasive and winning manner so as to evince the real Christian spirit of service to God and to man."[23]

The Tambaram conference generally supported the stance articulated by Kraemer but not without considerable debate and controversy. Kraemer framed the question of the relationship between the major religions in terms of a choice between those who saw a continuity between religions and those who identified a discontinuity between Christian revelation and the various religions. The majority present sided with Kraemer's discontinuity emphasis, but the debates made clear substantial differences on whether and to what degree God's revelation was manifested in the non-Christian religious traditions. Other discussions came at the issues from different angles. The Rev. E. Stanley Jones, a prominent American evangelist, for example, led a challenge against the "church-centered emphasis." He, and others, stressed the centrality of the Kingdom of God in relation to which the Church is relative. The Kingdom, he argued, places a demand on the whole of life—personal, devotional, economical, social and international. The emphasis on the Kingdom was more inclusive and, thus, allowed for more flexibility in addressing various concerns in an increasingly complex world.[24]

The debate among Christians on issues related to religious pluralism continued after Tambaram, but the primary concerns occupying the Western mission boards and people engaged in missionary work were practical ones stemming from complications related to World War II. Immediately after the war, however, Christians were challenged to reassess attitudes and relationships in the face of a religious resurgence in parts of Africa and Asia. Moreover, a host of new issues was introduced when numerous new nation-states were created in the late 1940s and early 1950s. The political reality of a post-colonial era added new impetus in the "disavowal of all spiritual imperialism" expressed by participants a quarter-century earlier in the Jerusalem conference.

In the 1950s, the newly established World Council of Churches (founded in 1948) formally explored interfaith issues. The Council's Departments of Evangelism and Missionary Studies, for instance, convened a four-day consultation among church leaders in 1955 for what was described as a *ballon d'essai.*

> The consultation revealed (1) that there is an increasing awareness of the need for fundamental study of the relationship of Christianity and the non-Christian religions, and (2) that a great deal more is required than the revival of an old debate (Tambaram) which had its own setting, terms and personalities, particularly in light of the greatly changed context of the meeting of religions and the recent developments in theological and biblical studies.[25]

These deliberations prompted the creation of a special project to study "The Word of God and the Living Faiths of Men." From the mid-1950s until 1971, various consultations, reports, and study papers examined different dimensions of the challenges and opportunities posed by the increasingly interdependent and pluralistic world. The processes were facilitated by the widely-read books published by scholars and church leaders. In the area of Christian-Muslim relations, Anglican Bishop Kenneth Cragg's writings, most notably his book *The Call of the Minaret*, signaled the serious effort to understand Islam on its own terms and, in the process, rethink traditional Christian positions.[26]

Several of the major international consultations convened by the World Council of Churches included active participation by representatives from the Vatican. In 1966, for instance, thirty

Catholic, Protestant, and Orthodox representatives spent a week in Brummana, Lebanon, discussing contemporary "Christian-Muslim Encounter." And again, in 1967, Catholic, Protestant and Orthodox leaders came together in Kandy, Sri Lanka, for an international meeting on the theme, "Christians in Dialogue with Men of Other Faiths." As the two major world bodies encompassing the large majority of Christians, both the World Council and the Vatican pursued the challenging interfaith agenda with their own programs and in consultation with one another.

Throughout this formative period in the 1950s and 1960s, the various initiatives continued to grapple with foundational theological concerns. The desire to understand, appreciate and engage neighbors from other traditions and to work cooperatively on common human problems became increasingly clear. What were not so clear were the theological moorings required in the midst of religious pluralism.

Critics of the enterprise maintained strong positions affirming traditional, exclusivist theology. The strongest opposition to dialogue or accommodation comes from Western fundamentalist Christians, many of whom are well-financed and highly visible. Muslims in the United States continue to find strong anti-Islamic sentiment among these fundamentalists. Rather than tolerance they perceive a "crusader" mentality or a subordination reminiscent of colonialism. Several Muslim friends have registered their complaints, noting that Islam is often singled out as unacceptable or dangerous—even by people who are otherwise tolerant.

Many, but by no means all, of the Christians at the forefront of the interfaith initiatives have lamented the absence of adequate theological frameworks, ones that maintained biblical integrity but expanded beyond the limits of a rigidly exclusivist position. The challenging agenda put forward for the programs of the Vatican and World Council—and for Christians who recognized the urgency of the inquiry—included the search for a more adequate theological framework within which to live out the life of faith in a world of great religious diversity.

During the past quarter-century, many people have taken up the challenge. In the next chapter, we will highlight efforts to understand key biblical texts, survey the three primary ways in which contemporary theologians are responding to pluralism and, finally, look at one major scholar who has applied his thinking to some particular concerns in Christian-Muslim relations.

CHAPTER FOUR

Christian Particularity
and Religious Pluralism:
Biblical and Theological Options

Genuine awareness of religious diversity coupled with the recognition that each of us occupies only one place on a rather large spectrum — even within our own religious community — is unsettling. The realization raises serious questions about one's worldview and belief system. Although the issues arise in different ways and at different times, most people can identify initial life experiences or situations in which they became aware of the complexity involved. The importance of uncontrollable factors, such as the location and cultural context into which one is born, also challenge unstated assumptions. In my case, I am aware that being born in Tulsa, Oklahoma, as opposed to Cairo or Banaras made a great deal of difference in the formation of my worldview and belief system. Unlike past centuries, however, it is increasingly difficult to slip back into a comfortable parochialism after such matters have surfaced. While the act of faith and the intentional decision to follow Christ transcend the accident of birth, we cannot escape the ever-present reality of pluralism. The questions posed demand thoughtful responses.

Christians instinctively turn to the Bible for insights and guidance when confronted with confused or conflicting issues related to the life of faith. What exactly does the Bible teach about God's activity in the world beyond the church? beyond the Jewish religious community? Do the Bible and the Christian religious tradition provide answers or at least an orientation for the nagging questions related to faith in a world of such diversity? My own plunge into biblical exploration was aided by several thoughtful church leaders and teachers. Although some mentors had gone a long way toward resolving major elements of these issues in their own minds, I was fortunate that they did not try to impose answers on me. To a person, they respected the importance of the inquiry for me and sought to facilitate it. They were wise enough to know that quick and easy answers to nettlesome, multidimensional theological questions of such consequence were ultimately unsatisfactory.

THE BIBLE AND RELIGIOUS PLURALISM

The first discovery is that the Bible presents more than one perspective. Anyone looking for simple, unambiguous answers in the Bible can certainly find them. But the prooftext approach requires selective reading and simplistic interpretation. Wrestling with seemingly different affirmations may not be easy, but it is the most honest and, in the long run, rewarding approach.

Looking first at the relationship of Christianity to Judaism, one finds a complex picture. The identification with the Jewish tradition was so pervasive that many early believers were reluctant to extend the evangelical mission to the gentile world. The necessity of maintaining Jewish practices, such as circumcision, provoked considerable internal debate. The decisive break beyond the confines of the church's Jewish origins came in the ministry of Paul. But, even with Paul, the Jewish-Christian dynamic was not simple.

Paul, a zealous Jew whose vocation expanded to embrace the new Christian faith, gave his life to the conviction that God's saving grace is manifest and mediated through the life, death, and resurrection of Christ. For Paul, the gospel of Christ is directed not only to the Jews, but to the gentile world as well. Even so, within the Pauline corpus there remains an affirmation that God continues to relate to the Jewish people. In Romans 9–11, Paul sets forth the view that Jews remain beloved in God's eyes, "for the gifts and the calling of God are irrevocable" (Rom

11:29). Paul continues by quoting the prophet Isaiah, who poses a question that gives pause to anyone who is certain that he or she has the market on truth cornered:

> O the depth of the riches and wisdom and knowledge of God! How unsearchable are his judgments and how inscrutable his ways! For who has known the mind of the Lord? Or who has been his counselor? (Rom 11:33–34)

Within the biblical materials, there are strong indications that God's active involvement in creation extends well beyond the bounds of Israel and the church. Acts 14:16–17 declares that God has allowed all the nations to walk in their own ways, yet God "has not left himself without witness." The story of Cornelius (Acts 10) illustrates both this reality and the difficulty involved in accepting a broader, less exclusive understanding.

Cornelius, a centurion, is described as a "devout," "God-fearing," "upright" man who "prayed constantly to God" and "gave alms liberally" to the poor. The account in Acts reports that Cornelius was directed by a "holy angel" to send for the Apostle Peter. Peter comes to Cornelius's house. His first utterance is a reminder to those present that it is "unlawful for a Jew to associate with or visit a Gentile." Peter's reticence is overcome by God whom Peter claims has shown him that he "should not call anyone profane or unclean." Cornelius relates how an angel told him that his prayers had been heard and his almsgiving had been remembered before God and that he should send for Simon Peter. Then, in an astonishing theological statement, Peter declares: "I truly understand that God shows no partiality, but in every nation anyone who fears him and does what is right is acceptable to him" (Acts 10:34–35). Peter then proceeds to proclaim the gospel to those assembled in Cornelius's house.

The account recorded in Acts is fascinating from several angles. Not only is it a clear statement of God's active involvement beyond the confines of Israel and the church; it also illustrates how difficult it is to expand one's theological horizons. Peter, the cornerstone in the foundation of the church, feels obliged to announce his reluctance at even coming to the house.

It is only his sense of God's directive that prods him to be there. In the process of the encounter, the insight comes to Peter. His eyes are opened and he sees the inadequacy of his theological understanding. The reader or hearer of the story can almost feel Peter growing and stretching as he apprehends new ways that God is at work in the world. It is heartening as well as humbling to realize that Peter, a disciple who had walked with Jesus, a man who was a leader among the leaders of the early church, could be changing so dramatically in his theological understanding at this late stage of his ministry.

There are other indications in the New Testament that God's love extends to all of creation and that God desires the salvation of all humankind (e.g., Rom 2:6–7; 1 Tim 2:4; Acts 14:17). Similarly, in the Hebrew scriptures one discovers numerous examples of God's active engagement with people outside of Israel. The first eleven chapters of Genesis record God's activity among the nations. Following the account of the great flood, Genesis 9:8–17 tells of God's universal and unconditional covenant with all human beings and living creatures. In the stories about Abraham, there are intriguing references: in Genesis 14:18–19, the strange figure of Melchizedek, "a priest of the Most High," blesses Abraham; in Genesis 20, we read of God's intervention with Abimelech, the King of Gerar. Other biblical figures such as Jethro, Moses' father-in-law, and Pharaoh's daughter are described as non-Israelite people motivated by God. The entire book of Job takes place outside the nation of Israel. The sailors in the Jonah story are described as "calling upon the name of the Lord." All of these strands seem to connect in the declaration found in the final book of the Hebrew Bible:

> For from the rising of the sun to its setting my name is great among the nations, and in every place incense is offered to my name, and a pure offering; for my name is great among the nations, says the Lord of Hosts. (Malachi 1:11)

While there is considerable reason to look beyond the confines of Israel and the church to discover evidence of God's creative and redeeming hand at work, the Bible is not a book about comparative religion. The obvious focus in the Hebrew scriptures is on the people of Israel; the New Testament bears witness to the unique activity of God in Jesus and the early Christian understandings of the resurrected Christ. Although there is an element of exclusivity in the notion of Israel as the chosen people, Jews have not traditionally understood their corporate role as the only people in relation to God. Rather, their spiritual responsibility is to be "a priestly kingdom and a holy nation" (Ex 19:6) and thereby a light unto the nations. Through the people of Israel, all the people of earth will be blessed (Gn 12:3).

The New Testament, on the other hand, appears to present a much narrower and more exclusive understanding of the people of God. While the Christian gospel extends out to all people, most Christians have understood their scriptures to teach that salvation is achieved through Christ alone. Peter's statement in relation to Cornelius and other New Testament texts indicating God's loving, active concern for all creation notwithstanding, the majority view has found support in other well-known passages. Two of the most familiar texts are found in the Gospel of John and the Acts of the Apostles:

> Thomas said to him, "Lord, we do not know where you are going. How can we know the way?" Jesus said to him, "I am the way, the truth and the life. No one come to the Father but by me. . . ." (Jn 14:5–6)

> And there is salvation in no one else, for there is no other name under heaven given among mortals by which we must be saved. (Acts 4:12)

These texts do not stand alone. The thrust of the New Testament bears witness to the unique and universal acts of God in Jesus. These particular passages, on the surface at least, proclaim succinctly the exclusive means for human salvation. How then can we reconcile this with broader, less restrictive affirmations in the Bible? Is it necessary to achieve such a reconciliation? Could these apparently contradictory theological positions both be true?

I vividly recall putting these and similar questions to a Southern Baptist pastor in the late 1960s. This pastor, who was the epitome of a zealous, evangelical Christian, surprised me and most of his immediate family when he responded by saying that we must never forget that God is far greater than our understanding of God. This man—who often led revival meetings and could not rest easily knowing that a particular Jewish friend (whom he had been proselytizing for fifteen years) had not accepted Christ—cited the scriptures he found most compelling. He conceded that it is very likely that God is working beyond the church in ways that we cannot begin to perceive or understand. But, he added, even though he was 95% sure that was the case—that is, that explicit faith in Christ was not the only means to salvation—he would continue to preach and teach the scriptures as he had for forty years. His rationale: I do know what God has done in Christ for me. My responsibility is to share that Good News. Even though I am 95% sure (based on biblical teachings alone) that God is drawing all manner of people unto himself, the 5% of uncertainty remains. In any case, whether the Christian faith is the only way or a primary way to salvation, he would stress that we must not relax in our responsibility to preach Christ.

This pastor, who apparently had not been quite this explicit with several of his own children before, went on to say I should continue my study and spiritual journey with faith in God and without fear of discovering new truths. It was a wonderful, liberating moment.

Since that time, I have understood that even a clearcut exclusivist position can and often does have soft, even flexible edges. Far too often, Christians on the more liberal end of the theological spectrum do not perceive the subtleties and sophistication present among more traditional and conservative evangelical Christians. People on all points along the spectrum differ not only on their theological perspectives, but on the way they project their views. Deep conviction need not be linked to cocksure arrogance or a condescending judgmental demeanor; it can be (I would argue, *should be*) accompanied by a sense of humility and openness to new insights. Gratitude for one's relationship with God or satisfaction with one's worldview is not enhanced by depreciating the experience and perspectives of those who differ—either within one's own tradition or beyond it. The words of Jesus recorded in John's gospel are helpful: "Do not let your hearts be troubled. Believe in God, believe also in me. In my Father's house there are many dwelling places; if it were not so, would I not have told you that I go to prepare a place for you?" (Jn 14:1–2).[1]

My friend, the Southern Baptist minister, did not feel compelled to try and reconcile different emphases in the New Testament. He was quite content to accept and proclaim John 14:6 and Acts 4:12 as literally true. Other Christians are not as comfortable living with the tension of the seemingly fundamental contradiction. Many are calling for and some are pursuing new ways to interpret these texts. Wesley Ariarajah and Kenneth Cracknell are among those who have offered alternative perspectives on some of the oft-quoted "exclusivist" passages in the New Testament. Neither wants to dismiss or simply explain away the texts. Rather, they argue that it is possible to discover new, deeper meaning in these familiar passages.

Dr. Ariarajah, a Methodist minister from Sri Lanka who has served on the staff of the World Council of Churches during the 1980s, stresses that the key to understanding is found in discerning the language of faith and love. He focusses on the Gospel of John, reminding us that the fourth gospel stands apart from the three synoptic gospels. The writer of John presents a more theological account of Jesus' life and ministry. He makes use of most of the incidents in the life of Jesus "to introduce theological discourses on the significance of Jesus to the faith community of his time."[2] Taking care not to overstate the distinction among gospel accounts, Ariarajah stresses that we must read the New Testament with an awareness that it presents a clear witness to the "Christ of faith."

What does this amount to? Does it mean that John, Paul and the author of the Letter to the Hebrews are not reliable guides to our understanding of who Jesus was? Does this mean that we must discount their testimony that Jesus is the Son of God, the Christ, the mediator, the way, the truth and the life? By no means. John, Paul, Peter and others are part of the Christian tradition; they tell us what Jesus meant to his immediate followers and to the early church ... What we should remember, however, is that these are all statements of faith about Jesus the Christ. They derive their meaning in the context of faith, and have no meaning outside the community of faith. They hold enormous significance for Christian people, today as in the past. They were absolutely valid for those who confessed Christ in centuries gone by, and they continue to be valid for those of us who belong to that tradition of confession. But we should not assume that these confessions were definitive.[3]

Ariarajah draws upon the "not entirely dissimilar" example of another historical person, Gautama Buddha, to illustrate the importance of understanding exclusive truth claims within their context of the faith commitment of the community. Although Gautama believed he had found a way to enlightenment for all human beings, he stressed that no one needed to know him or worship him to find *nirvana*. However, Gautama's followers saw in the Buddha far more than he apparently claimed for himself. Today, a large segment of the Buddhist community would reject flatly any suggestion that their veneration or worship of the Buddha is any sort of later accretion. Rather, they make their affirmation as an expression of the fuller understanding of who Gautama Buddha really was. For Christians who recoil at the comparison, Ariarajah simply asks that they consider how a Buddhist might view the distinction between the synoptic accounts of Jesus' life and early church confessional statements about the Christ. The parallels are not precise, but they are worth pondering.

One need not search out a Buddhist student of the New Testament to appreciate Ariarajah's point. Throughout much of this century, New Testament scholars and Christian theologians have endeavored to identify and understand the dynamic relationship between the historical Jesus and the Christ of faith. The ongoing, elusive quest for an adequate christology speaks to the difficulty involved in articulating the matter coherently.[4]

We begin to get clarity, in Ariarajah's view, when we recognize the different levels at which language is used and the different standpoints from which claims are made. He suggests the way forward is found when we untangle the notion of absolute truth and confessional statements uttered in the language of faith and love. He illustrates the distinction in a way all parents can readily understand.

> When my daughter tells me that I am the best daddy in the world, and there can be no other father like me, she is speaking the truth, for this comes out of her experience. She is honest about it; she knows no other person in the role of her father. The affirmation is part and parcel of her being. There are no doubts about it in her mind. She may be totally disillusioned if she is told that in fact her father is not the best daddy in the world.
>
> But of course it is not true in another sense. For one thing, I myself know friends who, I think, are better fathers than I am. Even more importantly, one should be aware that in the next house there is another little girl who also thinks her daddy is the best father in the world. And she too is right. In fact at the level of the way the two children relate to their fathers, no one can compare the truth content of the statements of the two girls. For here we are not dealing with absolute truths, but with the language of faith and love. . . .
>
> The language of the Bible is also the language of faith. . . . The problem begins when we take these confessions in the language of faith and love and turn them into absolute truths. It becomes much more serious when we turn them into truths on the basis of which we begin to measure the truth or otherwise of other faith-claims. My daughter cannot say to her little friend in the next house that there is no way she can have the best father, for the best one is right there in her house. If she does, we will have to dismiss it as child-talk![5]

Ariarajah anticipates strong objections from those who find his way of understanding dangerous in that it appears to relativize the faith. Surely, the counterargument goes, the truth of the gospel is independent of any given person's belief or experience; the uniqueness of Christ is a matter of fact, not just a confession of faith. Ariarajah, like my Southern Baptist minister friend, does not want to undermine the validity and life-changing importance of a Christian's relationship with God. However, both suggest that a measure of humility and restraint is required lest one project their experience of truth as absolute and binding for everyone else.

Ariarajah puts forth a dynamic, relational, and deabsolutized understanding of truth in simple and understandable terms. His approach provides a way to appreciate and affirm the centrality of the New Testament's confessional statements without solidifying the words into static, absolute, propositional truths.[6] Viewed from this angle, the declarations in John 14:6, Acts 4:12 and elsewhere are powerful and foundational truths in the experience of people of faith; they are not, however, necessarily bases for projecting an "exclusive" and rigid Christian theological framework onto the experience of all human beings.

Kenneth Cracknell, a Methodist scholar in England, approaches passages such as John 14:6 and Acts 4:12 in another manner. His argument, put forth in a detailed and thoughtful fashion, suggests that these texts ought not compel Christians "to the faith in Jesus Christ with a dogmatic exclusivity that leaves no place for other masters and other teachers." Rather, he suggests that these famous verses, if read in another way, are of "inestimable value to us in arriving at a Christian understanding of God's ways with his human children."[7] Cracknell sees these texts not as problematic, but as the centerpiece in an inclusive christology for religious pluralism. The main thrust of his interpretation goes as follows.

Cracknell draws heavily upon the insights of numerous biblical scholars in order to set the context for the exchange culminating in Jesus' declaration. He does this both by placing the Johannine materials into the setting of the Graeco-Roman world with its plethora of religious groups and by reflecting on the passage in view of the fourfold understanding of christology operative since the days of the early church. Recall that these words are uttered by one whom Christians understood as (1) one person who was at the same time (2) truly human, (3) truly divine, and (4) ultimately related to the action, presence, and revelation of God in human history (i.e., the *logos*). The history of how Christians have sought to hold all of these elements in proper tension is long and intricate. Cracknell wants us to maintain that tension, but especially to concentrate on the fourth element in this particular passage since the entire Gospel of John is developed in light of the *logos*.

Jesus' statement is set in response to questions posed by Thomas. In essence, Cracknell asserts, in John 14:5 Thomas is asking Jesus: What is your ultimate intention? How can others follow you in achieving your purpose? Cracknell, citing various scholars, warns the reader to avoid casually reducing these rich words to a set of simple theological propositions. He describes Jesus' answer as "majestic in its obscurity," linking redemptive suffering and life through death.

Jesus' reference to "the way" must have struck a chord in his hearers. The New Testament period included a multiplicity of religious ways and paths. Cracknell cites the imagery of a proper or salutory "way" or "path" as it is found in all of the major religious traditions. What is most striking in John, however, is the personalization by Jesus: "I am the Way." The way of Jesus—the path of rejection and suffering, of abandonment and death—was discontinuous with the teachings of others. In Cracknell's view, this unique, distinctive component must be interpreted in the context of the overarching theme of the *logos* in John. He then develops his christological understanding upon the premise that it is through the presence of the *logos* that "the way of God has been felt and apprehended in the created order as Romans 1:18ff makes clear." From this point, Cracknell argues that the various paths present in religious history have "inspired, consoled and encouraged the hearts of human beings" precisely because they are "immediately and directly in relationship to the One who is the Supreme dominating Way in the whole tumultuous movement of the world in progress."[8] He sums up his movement toward an inclusive christology with these comments:

> The Eternal Word is everywhere at work, creatively and redeemingly. He subsists eternally in God. He is that

hypostasis in the Godhead who goes forth in creation, in revelation and redemption. . . . If it is truly the case that all human beings are created in and through the eternal Word, the *logos*, we can hardly suppose that it can be the view of the author of the Fourth Gospel that because the Word has become flesh and lived among us, that primary relationship has come to an end. On the contrary, the argument must surely be "how much the more" are all human beings likely to be related to God through that One who is now risen and ascended.[9]

Cracknell's process of exegesis and interpretation is similar for what he calls "the other much-quoted 'exclusivist' text": Acts 4:12. While noting that the Lucan materials are not as rich theologically as the Johannine corpus, Cracknell concentrates on the narrative context. Coming in the flow of events recorded in chapters three and four, Peter's proclamation makes sense as a continuation of his appeal based on the healing miracles. The Greek noun and passive infinitive in Acts 4:12, usually rendered "salvation" and "be saved," respectively, carry the notion of healing and wholeness. In Acts 4:9, the same root is employed when Peter is discussing with the Jewish authorities the event recorded in Acts 3:6 (the healing of a man lame from birth). He cites the "good deed done to a cripple" and the "means by which this man has been healed." Cracknell suggests that a possible rendering of 4:12 might be the following: "There is no healing in any one else at all . . . there is no other name . . . by which we must be healed." The context indicates, in Cracknell's view, that Peter "is not making a general statement of universal validity." Rather, he is appealing to Jewish leaders that such a miraculous healing is reason for them to accept their Messiah. Cracknell prefers the more traditional translations, but urges a broader, less rigid interpretation of "salvation" in view of the context in Acts. In any case, he stresses that "there must be some doubt whether there are enough grounds here to deduce an exclusive doctrine about who is ultimately acceptable to God."[10]

In a final observation, the British scholar proffers a perspective akin to that of Ariarajah. He believes the declaration by

Peter, even if understood primarily in terms of salvation and not healing, reflects reality from the Christian perspective. For the Christian, there is no other name. Not wanting to relativize this truth, Cracknell suggests that Christians must, by definition, affirm the healing, salvific work of God through Jesus Christ. It is an affirmation; not necessarily a means to discern what God is not doing where the name of Jesus is not known.

Cracknell and Ariarajah are not alone. A number of scholars and church leaders are striving to provide new ways of understanding the New Testament passages that appear to present conflicting views on the universal activity of God in salvation. We can expect a variety of books and articles focussed on these central concerns during the coming decade. But, as Cracknell's exposition illustrates, considerable groundwork has already been done. The interested student can find a wealth of thoughtful and provocative material in the major biblical commentaries already in print. Individuals and study groups should not assume that any particular biblical verse can support the weight of a fully developed theology. Not only must we take seriously the scriptures as a whole, but, as these scholars suggest, we must endeavor to come to terms with the ambiguities and tensions arising in relation to questions of such monumental importance as those of religious pluralism.

OPTIONS FOR CHRISTIAN THEOLOGY

Virtually all people who count themselves as Christians have a theological perspective on religious pluralism. The views may be rooted in rigid doctrinal positions or unstated intuitive or experiential perceptions. They may not be well-defined or articulate, but the views exist. Ask five Christians at random whether or to what extent they believe it is possible for people of faith—Jews, Hindus, Buddhists, Muslims—to be in a meaningful, even saving relationship with God apart from an overt connection through Jesus Christ. The responses may well be different than expected—even if the different positions are not well substantiated.

As we have mentioned earlier, significant shifts have taken place among Christian scholars and leaders, particularly since the middle of this century. As appreciative understanding of other traditions has become more widespread, many Christians have offered sharp criticism of what they deemed to be Christian arrogance and imperialism. The changing dynamics present in the late 20th century have spurred a number of theologians to reorient and reshape their theological framework. One product of this process is what John Cobb calls "theological confusion."[11] Although the intentional focus on theology in a pluralistic world is relatively recent, a number of books and several excellent surveys have already appeared.[12]

Broadly, the most prominent alternatives can be grouped into three major paradigms or schools of thought. These positions are simply constructs that help to clarify major emphases among contemporary theologians. Considerable diversity exists, not only between the three, but also within each category. And the dividing lines are sometimes rather amorphous. Our purpose here is simply to introduce the range of options at present in the hope that the reader will reflect on her or his own perspective more self-critically.

The realization that thoughtful Christian theologians are far from united in their respective understandings of the meaning of pluralism for Christians should serve as an impetus to reassess one's views. The knowledge that the issues are too serious to rely on simplistic, jingoistic slogans or pat answers suggests the need for responsible study and deeper reflection. The process of plunging into the "theological confusion" may be disconcerting or liberating or both. For some, it may require adding a considerable amount of grey to a sharply defined worldview painted in black and white. For others, the recognition that their intuitive or experiential awareness is not necessarily in conflict with biblical perspectives may provide a great sense of relief and hope. Perhaps the parameters are not quite as fixed as traditional theological formulations would imply. The exploration and refinement of theological views can become a challenging and positive process. In any event, the reality is that subtle and sharp diversity is clearly visible among serious Christian thinkers whose basic orientation can be lodged within one of three major categories: exclusivist, inclusivist, and pluralist.

Exclusivism

The exclusivist position has been the dominant one over the centuries. It rests on the unshakable conviction that Jesus Christ provides the only valid way to salvation. The position draws upon the experience and confessional stance of the early church as reflected in the New Testament. Declarations such as John 14:6 and Acts 4:12 are appropriated as unambiguous and succinct statements to be taken literally. Apart from a deliberate confession of Christ, there can be no salvation.

There is, however, room for considerable mobility within this paradigm. On one end there is the mechanical, literalist stance mirrored in the headline-grabbing words of the Rev. Bailey Smith: "God does not hear the prayers of the Jews." Mr. Smith, who uttered these thoughts from the platform of a National Affairs Briefing in Dallas while serving as president of the Southern Baptist Convention in 1980, later explained, "It is not that God doesn't want to hear the prayers of Jews . . . it is simply that He can't. Unless you pray in the name of Jesus, the prayer just cannot get through to God." Despite considerable criticism, Smith (and others) defended the position as a hard fact of life taught by the scriptures. They did not explain clearly, however, how God heard the prayers of Abraham, Moses, and David, or Cornelius (a gentile), or a host of others outside Israel and the church.

Smith and a number of other prominent evangelical leaders (some of whom are highly visible through their TV ministries or highly audible over the radio airwaves) operate with a given set of assumptions. From this end of the exclusivist spectrum, one detects little hard grappling with complex issues posed by human religious diversity. For religious authorities who place themselves at this place along the theological spectrum, the case is closed.

Other exclusivists, such as Karl Barth and Hendrick Kraemer, have labored mightily with the issues under consideration. Their conclusions have tended to rest on an understanding of Christian faith that sets it apart from all manner of religions — including Christianity. In this view, religions are marked by humankind's fundamental sinfulness and are, therefore, erro-

neous and frail constructs. However well-intentioned the religion may be, these scholars would argue that, ultimately, they
must be evaluated in the light of the unique revelation of God
in Jesus Christ.

Some in the exclusivist camp acknowledge the biblical teaching on revelation outside of Christ. However, living after the
events of the crucifixion and resurrection, they maintain that we
cannot know with certainty the extent to which general revelation and God's present activities are sufficient for salvation. So,
like my Southern Baptist pastor friend, some exclusivists conclude that we cannot know how (or even if) God saves people
who do not confess Christ. We must, in the end, leave such
matters to the wise mercy of God.

One also finds considerable latitude among exclusivists on
how Christians ought to relate to adherents of other religious
communities. On one end there are those who seek no meaningful interaction outside of an evangelistic missionary encounter. Others, such as Kraemer and the contemporary Scottish
Presbyterian, Lesslie Newbegin, reject this approach. Rather,
they affirm the need for practical cooperation, mutual tolerance,
and respect and open dialogue in which both partners are prepared to teach and to learn. It is important to recognize that
such concerns can be addressed without compromising or weak-
ening the fundamental orientation of the exclusivist position.

During the 1990s, we can anticipate the appearance of new,
more thoughtful and nuanced positions by theologians who consider themselves to be exclusivist, particularly as more writers
respond to the challenge presented in the inclusivist and pluralist positions.

Inclusivism

The inclusivist position is distinguished by its affirmation of
both the salvific presence and activity of God in all religious
traditions and the full, definitive revelation of God in Jesus
Christ. Alan Race, the Anglican chaplain at the University of
Kent, describes this dual affirmation as both an acceptance and
a rejection of non-Christian traditions, a dialectical "yes" and
"no."

On the one hand it accepts the spiritual power and depth manifest in them (other religious traditions), so that they can properly be called a locus of divine presence. On the other hand, it rejects them as not being sufficient for salvation apart from Christ, for Christ alone is saviour. To be inclusive is to believe that all non-Christian religious truth belongs ultimately to Christ and the way of discipleship which springs from him. Inclusivism therefore involves its adherents in the task of delineating lines between the Christian faith and the inner dynamism of other faiths.[13]

The inclusivist position seeks to understand and interpret the apparently conflicting perspectives lodged within the New Testament and present among Christians throughout church history. It may come as a surprise to discover that the parameters defined by the inclusivist position have characterized the official position of the Roman Catholic church, by far the largest Christian communion, since Vatican II in the mid-1960s.

The Second Vatican Council can be described as the Roman Catholic church's contemporary effort to understand itself in light of the challenges of the modern age. The process of introspection led to new formulations on the proper relationship with others in the human family. Three of the sixteen official documents of Vatican II deal explicitly with interfaith relations. The concerns are addressed most directly in "The Declaration on the Relations of the Church to Non-Christian Religions" (*Nostra Aetate*). Promulgated by Pope Paul VI on October 28, 1965, this resolution is divided into five sections. The first section calls upon the church to examine "with greater care the relation which she has to non-Christian religions." The oneness of the human family and "God's providence, evident goodness and saving designs" for all people are affirmed.[14]

The second section recognizes that various religions attempt "to calm the hearts of men by outlining a program of life covering doctrine, moral precepts and sacred rites." The Catholic church "rejects nothing of what is true and holy in these religions" since they often "reflect a ray of that truth which enlightens" all men and women.

The Church, therefore, urges her sons to enter with prudence and charity into discussion and collaboration with members of other religions. Let Christians, while witnessing to their own faith and way of life, acknowledge, preserve and encourage the spiritual and moral truths found among non-Christians, also their social life and culture.[15]

The document mentions the Hindu and Buddhist religious traditions specifically and, by implication, the multitude of smaller communities practicing traditional religious ways.

The third section deals directly with Christian-Muslim relations. The declaration announces a fresh perspective on the church's approach to the faithful adherents of the Islamic religious tradition.

The Church has also a high regard for Muslims. They worship God, who is one, living and subsistent, merciful and almighty.... They strive to submit themselves without reserve to the hidden decrees of God, just as Abraham submitted himself to God's plan ... they await the day of judgement and the reward of God following the resurrection from the dead. For this reason, they highly esteem an upright life and worship God, especially by way of prayer, alms-deeds and fasting.[16]

The document pleads with both Christians and Muslims to forget the "many quarrels and dissentions" of the past centuries, to make a "sincere effort to achieve mutual understanding" and jointly "to preserve and promote peace, liberty, social justice and moral values." It concludes with a long section focussed on Christian-Jewish relations and a shorter general appeal invoking the words of Peter and Paul, who urged the faithful to "conduct themselves well among the Gentiles (1 Pt 2:12)" and, so far as is possible, to "be at peace with all men (cf. Rom 12:18)."[17]

Another text adopted by the Second Vatican Council, *Lumen Gentium*, addresses the dogmatic constitution of the church. This document embraces the view that salvation is possible for people outside the visible church:

Those, who through no fault of their own, do not know Christ or his Church, but who nevertheless seek God with a sincere heart, and moved by grace, try in their actions to do his will as they know it through the dictates of their conscience—those too may achieve eternal salvation.[18]

This broad affirmation carries enormous importance for both Christian mission and initiatives in interfaith dialogue. The thrust of the Roman Catholic position as articulated through Vatican II shifted the emphasis dominant for centuries. It is quite different to encounter another person whom one believes is the object of God's redeeming love and—as a Muslim, a Jew, a Buddhist—on the way to salvation, than it is to engage someone whom one believes to be misguided and en route to eternal darkness or hell. In the mission and dialogue efforts subsequent to the Second Vatican Council, the Catholic church leadership has sought to embrace the larger human community with the guidance of this frame of reference. We will return to these efforts in the next chapter as we seek clarity on helpful ways forward in Christian-Muslim relations.

The most prolific and influential theologian to put forth the inclusivist position is Karl Rahner. As with other theologians, it is difficult, perhaps unfair, to summarize Rahner's views which have been developed in painstaking detail. In broad strokes, Rahner's four basic theses define the framework within which he fleshes out his theological position with subtlety and erudition.

Christianity understands itself as the absolute religion, intended for all men, which cannot recognize any other religion beside itself as of equal right. . . .

A non-Christian religion . . . does not merely contain elements of a natural knowledge of God. . . . It contains also supernatural elements arising out of the grace which is given . . . on account of Christ. For this reason a non-Christian religion can be recognized as a lawful religion. . . .

Christianity does not simply confront the member of an extra-Christian religion as a mere non-Christian but as someone who can and must already be regarded in this or that respect as an anonymous Christian. . . .

[The Church is the] historically tangible vanguard and the historically and socially constituted explicit expression of what the Christian hopes is present as a hidden reality even outside the visible Church.[19]

For Rahner and a host of others who share elements of this inclusivist position, Christianity is unique and definitive; it is not, however, an exclusive club whose members are the only ones able to realize salvation. It is the "ordinary" path among an array of "extraordinary" paths visible in the world.[20] Like the exclusivists, inclusivists underscore the unambiguous finality of the universal presence and activity of Christ, the *logos*. They differ dramatically in their ways of understanding the dynamics and efficacy of the salvific power of Christ throughout human history.

As with other theological positions, the parameters for an inclusivist position are not fixed. For instance, many who might be considered inclusivists now avoid Rahner's term "anonymous Christians." Others stress the danger of focussing too much on "religions," insisting rather that it is God who saves people. Some suggest that religious traditions are social and symbolic manifestations of the divine-human encounter. As such, they are vital vehicles for inspiration and revelation, but they don't save people.

A famous line attributed to William James says, "I may not be able to define religion, but I know it when I see it." So, too, an inclusivist theology. While it is not easily defined, it was unmistakably visible in the reflections of John Paul II following the "World Day of Prayer for Peace" in Assisi (October 1986). Speaking to a gathering of cardinals and representatives of the curia, the pope said the following:

The World Day of Prayer for Peace at Assisi . . . seems to have been the *religious event* that attracted the greatest attention in the world in this year. . . .

Indeed, on that day, and in the prayer which was its motivation and its entire content, there seemed for a moment to be even a visible expression of the hidden but radical unity which the divine Word, "in whom everything was created, and in whom everything exists" (Col 1:16; Jn 1:3), has established among men and women of this world. ... The fact that we came together in Assisi to pray, to fast and to walk in silence—and this, in support of the peace which is always so fragile and threatened, perhaps today more than ever—has been, as it were, a clear sign of the profound unity of those who seek in religion spiritual and transcendent values that respond to the great questions of the human heart, despite concrete divisions. ...

The divine plan, unique and definitive, has its centre in Jesus Christ, God and Man, "in whom men find the fullness of their religious life, and in whom God has reconciled all things to himself" (*Nostre Aetate*, 2). Just as there is no man or woman who does not bear the sign of his or her divine origin, so there is no one who can remain outside or on the margins of the work of Jesus Christ who "died for all" and is therefore the Saviour of the world (cf. Jn 4:42). ...

The Day of Assisi, showing the Catholic Church holding the hands of brother Christians, and showing us all joining hands with the brothers of other religions, was a visible expression of these statements of the Second Vatican Council. With this day, and by means of it, we have succeeded, by the grace of God, in realizing this conviction of ours, inculcated by the Council, about the unity of the origin and goal of the human family, and about the meaning and value of non-Christian religions—without the least shadow of confusion or syncretism. ...

One must say also that the very identity of the Catholic Church and her self-awareness have been reinforced at Assisi. For the Church—that is, we ourselves—has understood better, in the light of this event, what is the true sense of the *mystery* of unity and reconciliation which the Lord has entrusted to us, and which he himself carried out first, when he offered his life "not for the people only, but also to unite the children of God who had been scattered abroad" (Jn 11:52).[21]

Pluralism

A third paradigm, the pluralist, differs from the previous two most visibly at the point of christology. Advocates of pluralist theologies of religion see Christianity neither as the only means to salvation nor as the fulfillment of other religious traditions. Rather, the pluralist position affirms the viability of various paths.

John Hick, whom Knitter rightly identifies as "the most radical, the best known, and therefore the most controversial"[22] proponent of this position, calls for nothing less than a Copernican revolution in our theological thinking. Using a striking analogy from astronomy, Hick makes his case for a theocentric approach. The Copernican view of the sun as the center around which the planets orbit supplanted the Ptolemaic thesis which placed the earth at the center of the universe. Similarly, Hick argues, we need to "shift from the dogma that Christianity is at the centre to the realisation that it is God who is at the centre, and that all religions . . . serve and revolve around him."[23]

Hick, raised in the tradition of evangelical Christianity, spent fifteen years living and teaching in the multireligious setting of Birmingham, England. Since 1982, he has been on the faculty at the Claremont School of Theology in California. His numerous books and articles reflect a serious and prolonged study of the world's religious history. He develops his theocentric position in which the world's religious traditions are understood as "different human responses to the one divine Reality."[24] The distinctions among religious communities, according to Hick, arise largely through perceptions conditioned by historical and cultural circumstances.

This is not to say that Hick regards the differences between religious traditions as inconsequential. He recoils at the charge, sometimes uttered casually by critics, that his position is nothing more than relativism. Rather, he is persuaded that the varying human responses to the divine Reality are not the same. Substantial limitations, not the least of which are those bound up with the finitude of human experience and knowledge, conspire to produce markedly different religious expressions. For Hick, admitting that human religious experience and behavior are relative in the context of the true divine Reality, is not the same as saying all religious experience and behavior are essentially the same. Through creative encounter and dialogue, he believes adherents in the different communities of faith can grow in their understanding of the Reality that inspires all creation and come closer to realizing the moral and ethical ideal present in their respective traditions.

Wilfred Cantwell Smith, an Islamicist and historian of religion, provided an influential frame of reference for Hick and others with his study on *The Meaning and End of Religion*. Smith challenges the basic notion that there are self-contained entities called "religions." Through both an etymological study of the use of the term and an analysis informed by a striking knowledge of human religious history, Smith demonstrates the inadequacy of the "religions" as a category. Rather, he argues that human "faith" and the "cumulative tradition" better describe the dynamic interaction in religious experience. And, he illustrates various ways in which the traditions interact. Rooted in this historical approach, Smith has endeavored more recently to define the parameters for a world theology.[25]

Hick, Smith, and others who advocate a theocentric approach stand apart from exclusivists and inclusivists most sharply at the point of christology. Their positions require clarity on how Christians can embrace Christ as the unique savior without necessarily assuming that the experience of God is mediated to everyone else in the same way. The theologians within the pluralist paradigm do wrestle with this central issue, though their various formulations have begun only recently to be understood and critiqued.

Two recent volumes published in the "Faith Meets Faith" series of Orbis Books reflect the growing breadth and depth of interest in pluralism. In *The Myth of Christian Uniqueness: Toward a Pluralistic Theology of Religions*, twelve scholars explore historico-cultural, theologico-mystical and ethico-practical dimensions of religious pluralism. In the Preface, Paul Knitter spells out the underlying premise for the entire collection:

Insofar as it might be misleading, the title of this book makes its point. We are calling "Christian uniqueness" a "myth" not because we think that talk of the uniqueness of Christianity is purely and simply false, and so to be discarded. Rather, we feel that such talk, like all mythic language, must be understood carefully; it must be interpreted; its "truth" lies not on its literal surface but within its ever-changing historical and personal meaning. This book, then, rather than intending to deny Christian uniqueness, wants to interpret it anew.[26]

A second collection challenges the emerging notion of a pluralist paradigm. The title makes the point, playing on the title of the earlier Hick/Knitter volume: *Christian Uniqueness Reconsidered: The Myth of a Pluralistic Theology of Religions*. In this text, fourteen Christian scholars grapple with different aspects of pluralism under three headings: The Trinity and Religious Pluralism; Christ and the Religions; and Hermeneutics, Epistemology, and Religious Pluralism. The various essays illustrate the fluidity of categories and they stake out areas for future theological reflection among Christians who do not embrace a strictly exclusivist stance.[27]

In the final decade of the twentieth century, the theological debate on the meaning of Christian faith in a religiously plural world will intensify. The quality of the discussion and clarity on emerging perspectives will depend not only on the insights among scholars and theologians, but also on the contributions from people of faith living self-consciously in the midst of pluralism.

A NON-EXCLUSIVIST APPROACH TO ISLAM

The current efforts to reflect anew on the Bible and religious pluralism and to develop and refine theological frameworks provide the broader context within which more specific questions can be considered. The various ways Christians are today engaging the Hindu, Buddhist, Shintoist, Jewish, and other traditions cannot be summarized since the issues raised and points of convergence and divergence differ widely. When we turn the focus onto Islam, we again find considerable diversity even on what questions should be addressed. It is instructive, however, that a lively discussion exists. The traditional view that Islam must be false or woefully inadequate by definition since it is post-Christian is now being challenged. Hans Küng is among the more formidable voices calling for a nonexclusivist understanding of Islam.

Küng, a prolific, controversial, and highly influential Christian theologian, has written about many aspects of Islam and Christian-Muslim encounter in recent years. His comments on three basic questions reflect the orientation of his inclusivist (some might say "pluralist") perspective. His views may not satisfy people across a wide spectrum, but they do stimulate our thinking. In addition, his remarks remind us that a new day is dawning, a day in which new responses to issues of religious pluralism are both possible and necessary. The three questions are: Islam: A way of salvation? Muhammad: A prophet? The Qur'an: God's Word?[28]

Can Islam be understood as a legitimate means to salvation? Küng says yes. He calls attention to the normative position in the Catholic church since the Second Vatican Council. The church is no longer bound rigidly by the longstanding dogma *extra ecclesiam nulla salus* (there is no salvation outside the church). Küng emphasizes this dramatic shift in the largest Christian community since the teaching remains a relatively well-kept secret—even among Catholics! Further, Küng poses the question and offers his response as a means to challenge other churches to face the issue squarely. He rightly observes that the World Council of Churches has deftly avoided responding to this question since there is considerable disagreement among its 312 member communions.

If we are able to distinguish between the "ordinary" (Christian) way of salvation and the "extraordinary" (non-Christian) ways of salvation, Küng asks, what can be said about Muhammad? In Küng's view, Muhammad can no longer be dismissed in advance as most Christians have done through the centuries. Küng offers guidance by means of a fresh look at prophets in the Bible and a willingness to understand Muhammad in proper historical context.

Küng identifies seven parallels between Muhammad and the prophets of Israel:

—Like the prophets of Israel, Muhammad based his work not on any office given him by the community (or its authorities) but on a special personal relationship with God.

—Like the prophets of Israel, Muhammad was a strong-willed character, who saw himself as wholly penetrated by his divine vocation, totally taken up by God's claim on him, exclusively absorbed by his mission.

—Like the prophets of Israel, Muhammad spoke out amid a religious and social crisis. With his passionate piety and his revolutionary preaching, he stood up against the wealthy ruling class and the tradition of which it was a guardian.

—Like the prophets of Israel, Muhammad, who usually calls himself a "warner," wished to be nothing but God's mouthpiece and to proclaim God's work, not his own.

—Like the prophets of Israel, Muhammad tirelessly glorified the one God, who tolerates no other gods before him and who is, at the same time, the kindly Creator and merciful Judge.

—Like the prophets of Israel, Muhammad insisted upon unconditional obedience, devotion, and "submission" (the literal meaning of "Islam") to this one God. He called for every kind of gratitude toward God and generosity toward human beings.

—Like the prophets of Israel, Muhammad linked his monotheism to a humanism, connecting faith in the one God and his judgment to the demand for social justice: judgment and redemption, threats against the unjust, who go to hell, and promises to the just, who are gathered into God's Paradise.[29]

Küng reminds us that the New Testament speaks of "authentic prophets who came *after* Jesus: men and women who attested to him and his message, who interpreted and translated it for a new age and a new situation." In 1 Corinthians, the "prophets" occupy the second rank after the "apostles." Although the prophetic office largely disappeared after the second century, Küng insists that "the New Testament doesn't bid us reject in advance

Muhammad's claim to be a true prophet *after* Jesus."[30]

When he shifts to an historical perspective, Küng is persuaded that certain affirmations are irrefutable: the people of seventh-century Arabia were justified in listening to Muhammad's voice; they were lifted out of polytheism into monotheism; they received a boundless supply of inspiration, courage, and strength for their religious life through the words uttered through their prophet.

> For the men and women of Arabia, and, in the end, far beyond, Muhammad truly was and is *the* religious reformer, lawgiver, and leader: *the* prophet, pure and simple. Actually, Muhammad, who always insisted he was only a human being, is more than a prophet in our sense for those who follow in his footsteps: He is the model for the kind of life that Islam wishes to be.[31]

Having said all of this, Küng concludes by conceding that the relationship between Jesus the Messiah and Muhammad the Prophet has yet to be explained in detail. Even so, the ability to affirm or, at least, consider positively the legitimacy of his role as a prophet is a major breakthrough. The consequences for such openness will be evident at many levels, not least of which is a new consideration of the message recorded in the Qur'an.

Küng offers several comments in reply to the question, "The Qur'an: God's Word?" He acknowledges his indebtedness to W.C. Smith, who suggested in the mid-1960s that the two traditional responses ("yes," by Muslims; "no," by Christians and others) were adequate and functional so long as there was little co-mingling among the communities. People of faith who live in the contemporary, interdependent world community must necessarily revisit such questions and labor to respond with more subtlety and nuance. For Christians, the response should reflect an appreciation of the role of the Qur'an in Islamic (and the larger human) history; for Muslims, the question surfaces a host of historical-critical issues heretofore not considered relevant in relation to the Qur'an.[32]

Küng challenges those who would dismiss the Qur'an on the basis of the negative statements in the Bible concerning "the errors, darkness, and guilt of the non-Jewish or non-Christian world." He suggests that such texts are "aimed at people who culpably reject the biblical message." A more fruitful approach, in Küng's estimation, is found in biblical materials that reflect God's pervasive presence in all of creation: Romans 1-2 on the general revelation of God in nature; the affirmation in Acts that God has not left people without a witness to God; and the understanding of the divine *logos* in the Gospel of John.[33]

Küng avoids a direct answer to his question about the Qur'an. He readily acknowledges that Islamic history leaves no doubt that the Qur'an has been and is an effectively inspired and inspiring book. It is another matter, however, to affirm what Muslims affirm, namely: the Qur'an is the verbally inspired Word of God and, as such, is absolutely perfect "from every standpoint—linguistic, stylistic, logical, historical, scientific." Rather, he tables the question in anticipation of a long-term discussion within Islam, a discussion Küng believes must include the importance of historical-critical methods in Qur'anic study.

Growing awareness of religious diversity has inspired new efforts in biblical study and theological reflection among an increasingly wide spectrum of Christians. The efforts to articulate authentic Christian perspectives informed by more accurate and appreciative knowledge of the religious traditions—including our own—will continue to be a primary focus for the foreseeable future. The challenge does not reside only or even primarily with professional theologians and scholars. For many, the process of engaging others—a daily experience in our interdependent world—is a crucial element informing theological understanding.

For the past quarter-century, concerted efforts to facilitate constructive interfaith encounter have been pursued through focussed dialogue. In the next chapter, we examine the dialogue movement both to understand it better and to seek more clues in the search for a way forward in Christian-Muslim relations.

CHAPTER FIVE

The Dialogue Movement

During the past quarter century, the two largest global Christian institutions—the World Council of Churches (WCC) and the Roman Catholic church—have initiated programs for interfaith dialogue. In both cases, Christian-Muslim dialogue constitutes a major component of the overall endeavor. These institutional dialogue programs mark the beginning of a new chapter in the history of interreligious relations.

Several motivations have prompted the organized dialogue movement. These include the desire to foster understanding, stimulate communication, correct stereotypes, explore similarities and differences, and facilitate means of witness and cooperation across religious lines. Translating these concerns for better communication, mutual understanding and cooperation between Muslims and Christians into reality has proven to be no small task. The obstacles we have examined in earlier chapters—the long history of enmity, biased and inaccurate information and fundamental theological disagreements among and between Christians and Muslims—have been and continue to be formidable.

The newness of the enterprise and the absence of conceptual clarity on how best to organize and structure interfaith dialogue did not dissuade the WCC or Vatican leadership. Both ventured forward with the conviction that the demands of the gospel and those of global interdependence required new, more constructive relationships among religious groups. Both the WCC and the Vatican proceeded with the hope and expectation that the process of encounter would itself help shape the appropriate agenda.

The effort to understand and assess the organized dialogue movement is hampered by the ambiguity associated with the term "dialogue." The wide range of concerns drawn together under the umbrella of "dialogue" often create confusion. Thus, we must first spell out what we mean by dialogue before we turn to the specific activities of the WCC, Vatican, and selected initiatives in North America.

WHAT IS "DIALOGUE"?

Dialogue, by definition, is a conversation, a process of communication through speech. It is a reciprocal relationship in which two or more parties endeavor both to express accurately what they mean and to listen to and respect what the other person says, however different her or his perspective may be. But dialogue is more than an exchange of views. In a fundamental sense, it is a perspective, a stance, an openness. Dialogue represents a way of relating, even if the openness and vulnerability are not fully reciprocated. Ideally, mutuality in dialogue is present in communication, trust, understanding, challenge, growth, and even spiritual development.

David Lochhead, a theologian at the Vancouver School of Theology, insists that a dialogical orientation is not only desirable, but an imperative for Christians.

To speak of the dialogical imperative is an abstract and "secular" way to speak of the commandment of neighborly love. To love one's neighbor as oneself is to be in a dialogical relationship with one's neighbor. More specifically, the New Testament puts the command in striking form: we are to love our neighbors *as God has loved us*.[1]

This orientation is fundamental to Christian discipleship. But, as even the casual observer of human nature knows, the intention or capacity to live out what is right is often mitigated by less lofty elements of the human condition. Lochhead sums it up with these words:

> As with most calls to discipleship, we can find reasons for not following, and even when we do follow, the quality of our obedience leaves much to be desired. Our difficulty, however, is with the ambiguity of our lives, not with the call. The call to dialogue, to open, trusting and loving relationships with the neighbor, is clear and unambiguous. Dialogue needs no justification outside itself.[2]

While dialogue is its own justification, the experience of Christian history suggests the need for external help to focus "the ambiguity of our lives" and enhance "the quality of our obedience." The WCC and Vatican initiatives were designed, in part, as structured, institution-based programs to stimulate and foster a more visible manifestation of the discipleship informing a dialogical perspective. The leadership in both institutions have affirmed from the outset the immeasurable value of facilitating constructive, healthy interfaith encounter. Both have also underscored the need to focus the agenda for organized dialogue in order to move the encounter toward measurable goals.

Broadly defined, there are six types of dialogue: parliamentary dialogue, institutional dialogue, theological dialogue, dialogue in community/dialogue of life, spiritual dialogue and inner dialogue.[3] A few comments about these six types illustrate both their distinctive features and the interplay between them.

Parliamentary dialogue refers to the large assemblies created for interfaith discussion. The earliest example was the World Parliament of Religions convened in Evanston (near Chicago) in 1893. These types of meetings have become more frequent under the auspices of multifaith organizations such as the World Conference on Religion and Peace and the British-based World Congress of Faiths. The large international and multireligious gatherings organized by such groups do not lend themselves easily to a tightly focussed agenda. They tend rather to explore broader concerns such as the possibilities for better cooperation among religious groups, the challenges of peace and disarmament for people of faith, and so forth.

Institutional dialogue includes the organized efforts by particular religious institutions which aim at initiating and facilitating various kinds of dialogue. This type of dialogue also seeks to establish and nurture channels of communication between the institutional bases of other religious communities. This loosely defined category encompasses much of the work carried out through the WCC and, to a limited extent, the Vatican. Numerous variations of institutional dialogue are discernible at the local level. Among U.S. Catholics, for instance, diocesan-sponsored dialogue is frequently pursued by people serving on a team appointed by and representing the archdiocese.

Theological dialogue refers to particular elements found in interfaith encounter as well as the larger process of reflection among Muslims, Jews, Christians, Buddhists, and others. It includes structured meetings in which theological and philosophical issues are the primary focus of discussion. People from different traditions share information as well as explore commonalities and differences on anything from the nature of Ultimate Reality to the understanding of revelation to human responsibility toward God and the created order. Christians and Muslims, for example, may concentrate on their respective understandings of Jesus or the Spirit of God or the role of prophets and messengers in communicating God's revelation.

Theological dialogue also includes the wider contemporary discussion on the meaning of one's own religious tradition in the context of religious diversity and pluralism. Reflection on pluralism can be the focus for dialogue meetings; it is also a manifestation of insights gained, in part, through interfaith dialogue. Paul Knitter underscores this point when he suggests that dialogical encounter is pivotal for a Christian theology of world religions:

> My contention is that . . . interreligious dialogue can serve as a *hermeneutics of praxis* that will throw even greater light on . . . the central issues for any Christian theology of world religions: Is there revelation and salvation in other religions? What is the content and extent of such revelation? What is the place of Christianity among the religions of

the world? Is Christian truth the corrective, the fulfillment, of other religions?

I am suggesting that answers to such questions, like all answers, are not simply "given" in the Christian scriptures and tradition; they must be worked out through the praxis of dialogue. . . . To fashion a theology of religions outside the praxis of dialogue would be as inappropriate as it would be for a tailor to make a suit without taking the customer's measurements.[4]

Dialogue in community and the dialogue of life are inclusive categories that encompass most of the unstructured interaction between people of different traditions. Diana Eck, a specialist in Hindu studies at Harvard, has been an active participant in dialogue intiatives for many years. She describes this most prominent type of dialogue in the following manner:

Most interreligious dialogue takes place in markets and on street corners, at times of festivals or holy days, in the course of civic or humanitarian projects, at times of community or family crisis. It takes place as people in communities think together about violence, militarism, or economic depression; as they think about the marriage of their children or the community's responsibility toward the elderly.[5]

A primary function of organized dialogue meetings is to serve as a vehicle to stimulate and encourage more interaction in daily life. Organized dialogue may also concentrate on practical issues of common concern. Examples at the local level might include dialogue on the rights of religious minorities, issues arising from interreligious marriage, religious values and public education, and so forth. In addition, dialogue designed to facilitate common action in response to global issues like the plight of refugees or ecological problems may be classified as part of the dialogue in community.

Spiritual dialogue is concerned with deepening spiritual life through interfaith encounter. This type of dialogue does not struggle overtly with theological problems or issues between communities of faith. Rather, it is designed as a means to nourish, expand and develop spirituality or the spiritual dimension of religious life. As with other types, there is considerable latitude within the parameters of spiritual dialogue. The most conservative and nonthreatening approach might include observing the worship of others or hearing and sharing perspectives on the meaning of prayer in Christian, Buddhist, or Islamic spirituality. A more radical approach might include participation in joint worship experiences. The World Conference on Religion and Peace, for example, includes multireligious services as a part of its meetings, conferences and assemblies.

Thomas Merton was among the most visible and articulate Christians advocating spiritual dialogue. Merton, just prior to his untimely death in 1968, wrote the following:

> I am convinced that communication in depth, across the lines that have hitherto divided religious and monastic traditions, is now not only possible and desirable, but most important for the destinies of twentieth-century Man. . . . I think we have now reached a stage of (long-overdue) religious maturity at which it may be possible for someone to remain perfectly faithful to a Christian and Western monastic commitment, and yet to learn in depth from, say, a Buddhist or Hindu discipline and experience.[6]

The spiritual dialogue among monastics has developed substantially in the past three decades. Through a variety of conferences, monastic exchange visits and periodic meetings with the pope and other Vatican leaders, Christian and Buddhist monastics, in particular, have been exploring a heretofore largely unknown path.

A nonstructured but pervasive manifestation of spiritual dialogue is evident in the periodic popularity of different groups (Hare Krishnas, Zen Buddhists, Sufis) as well as the more recent New Age movement in the West. A visit to almost any large bookstore with a "Religion" section makes the point: scores of books on "Eastern Religions" and "mysticism" and "comparative religion" are prominently displayed.

While the popular and the more deliberate forms of dialogical exchange are rich and creative for many, they are viewed with considerable apprehension by many others. The process of learning about the spiritual life in other traditions is far less threatening than experimental efforts which involve crossing over into the experiential realm of another tradition. Thus, serious theological questions are lodged within the idea and practice of spiritual dialogue.

Finally, there is inner dialogue. This type of dialogue takes place in each of us. It is operative in various dialogical encounters as well as in our process of thinking and reflection. It is intimately bound up with growth and change and the development of one's religious perspectives. Diana Eck explains inner dialogue succinctly with these words:

> Inner dialogue ... is the dialogue that takes place in our minds and hearts when we read the Bhagavad Gita, when we meet a Buddhist monk or nun, when we hear the Muslim call to prayer, or when we share the Sabbath meal with Jewish friends. It is the inner dialogue that Gandhi experienced in reading the sermon on the Mount, and the inner dialogue Martin Luther King experienced in reading Gandhi. ... We are moved by our encounters with the other; we are attracted, we are repelled. We are gripped by the insights of the Bhagavad Gita, or by the prayers of the Muslim, and we wrestle with their meaning. The understandings that we gain cannot simply be put to one side, then, as we go about our life as Christians and think about the ultimate issues of life, and growth, and death that concern us as children of God. They become part of our own inner landscape, and they shape our continuing life as Christians.[7]

Most clergy have had the unsettling experience of rediscovering old sermons in their files and being mildly horrified at the way they viewed and presented particular issues five years ago or, perhaps, last year. All of us are constantly learning, changing, reshaping our worldviews. Admittedly, there are some people who believe and behave as though they have a lock on all truth and need not alter any perspective. But, in the end, no breathing human being with a functioning brain is really that static.

Inner dialogue is a normal process of human thinking and reflection. It is not, however, necessarily understood or embraced consciously, particularly when the inner dialogue concerns religious insights that challenge one's comfortable, existing positions. Organized dialogue seeks to awaken and nurture this self-conscious process of reflection.

That which separates dialogical encounter from two monologues is precisely the attitude, the openness, the orientation people bring to the encounter.

THE WCC PROGRAM FOR DIALOGUE WITH PEOPLE OF LIVING FAITHS

Following ten years of dialogue meetings, consultations and internal discussions, the WCC established the program subunit for Dialogue with People of Living Faiths and Ideologies (DFI) in 1971. Two decades later, the DFI continues its multifaceted program with new emphases and expectations conditioned by experience. The WCC program can be divided into three major components: organizing large international and smaller regional dialogue meetings; providing educational materials and working with churches to enhance understanding of other traditions; and facilitating Christian reflection on theological issues relating to pluralism.

The DFI has organized two major international Christian-Muslim dialogue meetings. The first brought together forty-six participants (25 Christians; 21 Muslims) from twenty countries for a week-long dialogue in Broumana, Lebanon in July 1972. Numerous presentations explored issues and options for improving mutual understanding and pursuing cooperation. The consultation produced a seven-page memorandum which spelled out the motivations, hopes, guiding principles, discoveries, and recommendations of those gathered. The discoveries included a need to temper expectations in the face of the abiding fears and mistrust between the communities. The recommendations centered on continuing the effort, particularly in the local settings to which the participants returned. There was also strong agreement on the need to nurture the dialogue movement within the respective communities. In all efforts, the importance of three guiding principles—frank witness, mutual respect and religious freedom—was affirmed. A brief passage from the memorandum conveys the sentiment at the gathering:

> We accepted that dialogue is not an attempt to suppress differences but rather to explore them frankly and self-critically. . . . Rather than being satisfied with a lowest common denominator, we faced up to sometimes poignant points of tension. Yet we also dared to hope for some convergence, not in impatient syncretism, but in openness to God's further guidance.[8]

Following a major multilateral dialogue meeting in 1974 and a period of intense internal debate, the WCC convened another Christian-Muslim dialogue in Colombo, Sri Lanka, in 1982. This consultation was an experiment, a deliberate effort to move beyond an affirmation of the need for cooperation in human service projects to actually developing concrete programs. Thirty-three Muslims came from 22 countries; 30 Christians came from 27 countries. In the end, the global gathering reflected more the reality of conflict than the promise of cooperation.

In the course of the meeting, the different expectations of those present became obvious. While many of the Christians were prepared to get out the maps, statistical charts, and finance sheets in order to begin planning for cooperation, most of the Muslims wanted first to resolve serious ethical and philosophical problems they perceived in the endeavors of certain Christian relief and rehabilitation organizations. Some Muslims chided Christian groups for what they felt was exploitation of the poor by using medical, educational, and relief assistance for the purpose of proselytization. The consultation scarcely got beyond the discussion about preparation and presuppositions of the participants. In the long run, it served an invaluable purpose by demonstrating vividly how deep and substantial are the differences—in perception and reality—between many Christians and Muslims.

The effort to move forward in cooperative programs was a

result of various WCC-related meetings in the 1970s. It was not only viewed as a tangible expression of new relationships, it was one of the primary places where Christians were united on the potential value of dialogue. Throughout the 1970s, considerable energy was devoted to internal Christian efforts to refine the nature and purposes of dialogue. The issues were joined in heated debate during the WCC's world assembly in Nairobi during 1975. Fears that dialogue would undermine Christian mission and fears over issues of theology and pluralism were voiced publicly at various points during the two-week assembly.

In direct response to Nairobi, the DFI organized a major international consultation in Chiang Mai, Thailand, in the spring of 1977. For nine days, 86 Orthodox, Catholic and Protestant leaders heard presentations, participated in both structured and unstructured discussions and shared in Bible studies. Their deliberations resulted in a substantial document ("Dialogue in Community") in which the most divisive and contentious issues were addressed: the relationship between dialogue, mission, and witness, the danger of syncretism and the theological significance of other traditions. The thoughtful text weaves its way through the thorny thickets, affirming the principles upon which the dialogue program was developed while, at the same time, identifying places where more study and reflection were needed. Chaing Mai was a crucial turning point for DFI and many WCC churches. It made clear that open dialogical encounter was not inhibited by the considerable diversity among Christians on dialogue/mission and theology of religions issues.

Chiang Mai set the stage for further internal reflection and production of materials for Christians interested in dialogue.[9] In December of 1979, 67 consultants traveled from 30 countries to join 27 Kenyans and seven WCC staff persons for a major consultation on "Christian Presence and Witness in Relation to Muslim Neighbours." The week-long meeting covered topics ranging from building community with Muslims to responsible mission, service, and dialogue. Tensions inherent in the imperatives of witness and dialogue were explored, if not resolved. In Mombassa, and in various other smaller WCC gatherings, mutuality in relationships was emphasized. That is, faithful Christians must, by definition, share the good news of the gospel. They must also appreciate the imperative for witness and proclamation on the part of Muslims. Each must approach and interact with the other in mutual respect.

Among many components, the Mombassa meeting featured biblical meditations and the sharing of personal stories from Christians who lived in predominantly Muslim lands. These contributions tended to endorse dialogue as a style of life. At the same time, the delegates stressed, once again, the need for further work in Christian theological reflection on religious pluralism, and Islam, in particular. The final declaration also made clear the necessity of more intentional dialogue on difficult topics such as the rights of minorities, women's issues, and the role of religion in political upheaval and change.

For most of the 1980s, the DFI program in Christian-Muslim relations focussed on regional rather than global meetings. These included a dialogue among youth convened in Geneva, a joint Europe/Middle East dialogue, a North American colloquium and an East Africa gathering in Tanzania. The shift toward regional meetings represented both the desire to focus on local concerns, as well as fiscal reality. Since the mid-1970s, the WCC has experienced a steady decline in income, and the grand scale international meetings characterizing the first phase of the DFI program were simply not feasible on a routine basis.

Twenty years after the institution of the DFI, it is still difficult to measure the "success" of the enterprise. The organized dialogue certainly has not realized the high expectations discernible in the early years. In retrospect, the agenda for DFI was far too ambitious and broad. Consequently, it has been difficult to sustain work on all aspects of the dialogue enterprise. Hopes for substantial progress in cooperation in human service ministries, for example, have not materialized. Further, the continual repetition of tentative or provisional statements and the need for further study and reflection on mission/dialogue and theological issues underscores the difficulty of achieving consensus among such a diverse group of churches.

Increasingly, the DFI has sought to zero in on issues and education within the Christian community. In 1986, for instance, the DFI initiated a two-year study program on "My Neighbor's Faith—and Mine." This adult education program not only presented dialogue and issues of pluralism in local congregations, it also attempted to measure "where the churches are" in their approaches and understandings. Predictably, the feedback from around the world revealed the diversity and ambiguity present among the churches. On balance, however, DFI staff and leaders were encouraged by the widespread engagement of churches with other people of faith and with issues of pluralism in their respective settings.

This study project, combined with a continuing call for more focussed theological reflection on pluralism within the WCC member churches, prompted the DFI to bring together twenty-five Protestant, Orthodox, and Catholic theologians for a special consultation in January, 1990. The participants sought to clarify positions on the universality of God's love for creation, the redemptive action in Jesus Christ, and the work of the Holy Spirit within and outside the church. While wide divergence exists among these theologians, a consensus may be emerging. In the view of Diana Eck, one of the participants, the final document produced by the consultation contains a "modified inclusivist view."

> There was profound agreement that God has found people, and people have found God, throughout human history and in the context of many religions and cultures. . . . It is in the sincere practice of their own faith that people come into relationship with God, not in spite of it. Here the consultation concurred. The final document insists that all religious traditions are ambiguous, in that religion has functioned to support "wickedness and folly" as well as its higher aims.[10]

The organized dialogue under WCC auspices seems best suited for academic and theological dialogue. Specific efforts at cooperation on community projects and experiments with spiritual dialogue have failed to yield tangible results. Most of the participants—Muslims and Christians—have been scholars or exceptionally well-educated and articulate leaders. Efforts to broaden the base of participation by including popular, even radical religious figures in such international gatherings have proven difficult. However, this limitation has not diminished the scope and importance of the DFI's role as a catalyst.

Without question, the World Council of Churches' dialogue program helped to launch a movement in the late 1960s and early 1970s. Reading the list of participants in the various meetings and tracking the activities of these people up to 1990 makes it clear that most have taken the idea and style of dialogue into all corners of the world. Several of the Muslim participants have written extensively on dialogue, mission, and the issue of religious pluralism within Islam. Most have been active in a host of interfaith activities at the local and regional levels.

Structured dialogue meetings have demonstrated their utility at several other levels. Over time, the content of meetings, the evaluation and planning processes, and the publication of resources have helped clarify issues. Dialogue challenges people to think and articulate their views clearly. In addition, meetings provide a context in which creative interaction takes place. Many of the participants, for example, have noted the importance of organized dialogue meetings for Muslim-Muslim and Christian-Christian interaction.

Institutional dialogue has limits. A structure like the WCC, for instance, is constrained by fiscal realities as well as a wide spectrum of constituency input. Moreover, when the WCC works with organizational partners in planning for and implementing a dialogue meeting, the constraints are multiplied. Having worked on the staff of a major ecumenical organization, I can attest to the difficulty imposed by bureaucratic structures with multiple interests.

The high expectations present when DFI was launched are still present among key actors within the churches. The sense of urgency and the hope for rapid movement forward in dialogue have given way to the realization that this is a long-term process. The experience of twenty years has helped Muslims, Christians, and others recognize both the value and limitations of institutional dialogue as one piece—albeit a substantial piece—in the larger picture of interfaith relations.

THE PONTIFICAL COUNCIL FOR INTERRELIGIOUS DIALOGUE

On Pentecost (May 17) in 1964, the new pontiff, Paul VI, established a Secretariat for Non-Christian Religions. Twenty-five years later (March 1989), in the reorganization of the curia, the secretariat was designated and renamed the Pontifical Council on Interreligious Dialogue (PCID).

Three months after the creation of the secretariat, Paul VI issued his first papal encyclical, *Ecclesiam Suam*. In this text, the pope went further than the Vatican Council when he spoke not only of persons but of other "religions." Islam was singled out for special mention among various traditions.

> We refer to the adorers of God according to the conception of monotheism, the Muslim religion especially, deserving of our admiration for all that is true and good in their worship of God. . . . Honesty compels us to declare openly our conviction that there is but one true religion, the religion of Christianity. . . . But we do, nevertheless, recognize and respect the moral and spiritual values of the various non-Christian religions, and we desire to join them in promoting common ideas of religious liberty, human brotherhood, good culture, social welfare and civil order.[11]

The mandate for the new secretariat concentrated on two primary tasks: studying the religious traditions and providing resources both for Christians and non-Christians; promoting interreligious dialogue through education and by facilitating efforts by bishops and others at the local level.[12]

In May, 1966, the secretariat began producing a periodical, *Bulletin*, as a way of disseminating information on and widening the circle for its work. In the latter part of the 1960s and early 1970s, the secretariat published a number of semi-official books of guidelines for dialogical encounter. Other publications reveal the close collaboration between the secretariat and Catholic institutions sharing related mandates. The Middle East and Asia staff with responsibility for Christian-Muslim relations, for instance, has a long history of cooperation with the Pontificio Istituto di Studi Arabi e d'Islamistica (PISAI). In addition to joint efforts on study seminars and programs in Rome, these staff have played a major role in the publication of two PISAI periodicals: the scholarly journal *Islamochristiana* (1975 to present); and the more popularly written, *Encounter — Documents for*

Muslim-Christian Understanding (1977 to present).

Under the leadership of Cardinal Pignedoli (1970-80), the secretariat placed a greater emphasis on more direct, personal contacts with Muslims, Hindus, Buddhists, and practitioners of traditional religious ways. In Christian-Muslim relations, the secretariat organized a number of visits and exchange meetings with Muslim government and religious leaders, including the Egyptian High Council for Muslim Affairs (1970), a delegation of Saudi jurists (1974) and representatives from the Indonesian Department on Religious Affairs (1977). They also worked closely with the WCC's Dialogue subunit and others in planning for and participating in a variety of regional and local consultations.

The work of the Vatican secretariat has had considerably higher visibility since the late 1970s as a result of the extensive travels and public statements by Pope John Paul II. In his first encyclical, *Redemptor Hominis*, the pontiff put forth his view that the action of the Holy Spirit is operative in the lives of non-Christians. He urged Christians to interact with adherents of other faith traditions through dialogue, contacts, and prayer. While the secretariat encourages and facilitates formal dialogue meetings, these always have been considered secondary. The primary concern, mirrored in *Redemptor Hominis*, revolves around the need to educate and stimulate people at the local level where the "dialogue of life" takes place.

In 1979, two new efforts to clarify the nature and importance of dialogue were undertaken. First, the Federation of Asian Bishops convened two Bishops' Institutes for Interreligious Affairs in Bangkok and Kuala Lumpur. These gatherings, called "BIRA I" and "BIRA II," concentrated on Christian-Buddhist and Christian-Muslim relations, respectively. In the statement issued at the conclusion of BIRA II, the bishops strongly endorsed the "dialogue of life" as the primary way the Catholic church understands dialogue with Muslims.

> The dialogue of life ... is the most essential aspect of dialogue, and it is accomplished by Christians and Muslims living together in peace. Each gives witness to the other concerning the values he has found in his faith, and

through the daily practice of brotherhood, helpfulness, openheartedness, and hospitality, each shows himself to be a God-fearing neighbor. The true Christian and Muslim offer to a busy world values arising from God's message when they revere the elderly, conscientiously rear the young, care for the sick and the poor in their midst, and work together for social justice, welfare, and human rights. We encourage Christians to be ever more deeply involved in this dialogue of life.[13]

The bishops conceded that many Christians feel they know very little about Islam and thus find it difficult to understand the practices and ideals of Muslims. What is required, then, is an even more concentrated effort to educate Christians for this dialogue of life.

The second initiative came when the Secretariat's Board of Members, a group of twenty bishops, launched a study process to help clarify the issues related to the most basic fears inhibiting dialogue. Although the Second Vatican Council declarations had modified the traditional understanding of mission, the finality and universality of salvation in Christ had not been reconciled clearly in official documents with the affirmation of God's action seeking out persons in all social and historical situations. The process, which included four revisions over five years, resulted in a substantial three-part statement that strives to maintain the integrity of both mission and dialogue and to make more explicit their intrinsic relationship. The final statement was promulgated by Pope John Paul II on the occasion of Pentecost, exactly two decades after the creation of the secretariat.

The document is organized under three subheadings: mission, dialogue, dialogue and mission. The thrust of the declaration on mission moves in the direction of a broader and more inclusive stance. The statement cites papal pronouncements and episcopal conferences in order to underscore the "complex reality of the totality of mission."

Mission is already constituted by the simple presence and living witness of the Christian life. ... There is also the concrete commitment to the service of mankind and of all forms of activity for social development and for the struggle against poverty and the structures which produce it. ... There is as well the dialogue in which Christians meet the followers of other religious traditions in order to walk together towards the truth and work together in projects of common concern. ... The totality of mission embraces all these elements.[14]

While holding firm on the centrality of proclamation and the call to Christian discipleship, the text cites the examples of Jesus, the early church and the lives of saints to stress the necessity for respecting each person's right to freedom of conscience. The foundation for dialogue with people of other faith traditions is based on personal and social needs:

As the human sciences have emphasized, in interpersonal dialogue ... a person discovers that he does not possess the truth in a perfect and total way but can walk together with others towards that goal. ... Religious experiences and outlooks can themselves be purified and enriched in this process of encounter. ... Socio-cultural changes in the world, with their inherent tensions and difficulties, as well as the growing interdependence in all sectors of society necessary for living together, for human promotion, and, above all, for pursuing the demands of peace all render a dialogical style of human relationships today even more urgent.[15]

The carefully crafted declaration emphasizes the teaching of *Redemptor Hominis* in which Pope John Paul II stated that Christ is united in some way with each person, whether or not the person is aware of it. This activity of God in the lives of all the people is the theological anchor for the Roman Catholic church as it pursues interreligious dialogue in different ways.

Four types of dialogue are identified, explained, and commended in the text. Followers of Christ, by reason of their human and Christian vocation, are responsible for cordial, respectful, and hospitable relations with others in the daily affairs of life. The "dialogue of life" is, above all else, "a manner of acting and a spirit which guides one's conduct." The second form of dialogue, the "dialogue of deeds," is expressed when Christians collaborate with others "for goals of a humanitarian, social, economic, or political nature which are directed toward the liberation and advancement" of humanity. Another form of dialogue is the "dialogue of specialists." In this context, selected persons with particular expertise are called together either to apply their knowledge to specific problems or to deepen and enrich their mutual understanding and appreciation of one another's spiritual values. Finally, the document speaks of the "dialogue of religious experience" as "a deeper level" where people rooted in their own religious traditions can share their experiences of "prayer, contemplation, faith, and duty, as well as their expressions and ways of searching for the Absolute."

The concerted effort expended in refining, producing, and disseminating these documents underscores the broad commitment to dialogue as a central activity for people of faith. While the Pontifical Council for Interreligious Dialogue takes the lead, the responsibility and urgency for dialogical encounter is a recurrent theme at the highest levels of the church leadership. Pope John Paul II routinely issues statements on special days in the Muslim (and Jewish, Hindu, Buddhist) religious calendar. He often meets with other religious leaders. Between 1980 and 1986, for example, the Holy Father met personally with Muslims on eighteen occasions. He normally includes interreligious harmony and cooperation as a priority when he addresses Catholic leaders visiting from various parts of the world. In addition, interfaith dialogue is a persistent theme in the pope's addresses to audiences during his extensive world travels. On one unprecedented occasion, August 19, 1985, the pontiff visited Morocco in order to address 80,000 Muslim youths at a stadium in Casablanca. The major themes in these various communications include an emphasis on common elements between the two religions, common concerns as humans with faith in God, the importance of Christian-Muslim dialogue, and the necessity for joint efforts to address social problems in our world.[16]

Perhaps the most dramatic expression of Pope John Paul II's interreligious concerns occurred in October 1986. In a highly publicized event, 108 representatives from the world's major religious communities and selected traditional religious groups gathered at the pope's invitation for a "World Day of Prayer for Peace" in Assisi. The leaders present joined in prayer, silent meditation, and fasting as they committed themselves to work fervently for a peaceful world. In a world torn asunder with innumerable local and regional conflicts—many of which have religious dimensions—this event offered a tangible sign of hope.

During the latter years of the 1980s and the start of the 1990s, many of the Vatican programs have been experimental in nature. After a period of documentation and developing educational materials, there is a new sense of openness and exploration visible in a multifaceted approach. Through an event like Assisi and in response to various local initiatives, the PCID is currently seeking to stimulate interreligious encounter at numerous levels.

While many Catholics in North America remain surprisingly unaware of the theological positions prevalent among their church leadership, a framework is being established. The multidimensional educational efforts carried out by the PCID, the teachings of the pope and numerous bishops worldwide provide a context for the ministry of the Catholic church (and attentive Orthodox and Protestant churches) in the pluralistic world that increasingly challenges traditional modes of thinking and behavior. The stated agenda of the Catholic leadership includes both the call to and preparation for the "dialogue of life" as primary concerns for people of faith. The "success" of the various endeavors comprising this agenda may not be possible to measure with any degree of confidence in the short run. Even so, viewed from the perspective of two thousand years of church history, the intentional focus on understanding and cooperation across religious lines represents a dramatic new departure in the orientation of the largest Christian communion.

INTERFAITH INITIATIVES IN NORTH AMERICA

One measure of the influence of the interfaith work carried out through the WCC and Vatican is found in the rapid growth and proliferation of interfaith activities in North America. If not directly influenced by the worldwide Christian institutions, the numerous groups at least testify to the growing awareness that interreligious understanding and constructive coexistence are required for the future of our society.

Parallel to the WCC and Vatican, there are distinct programs in Christian-Muslim relations carried out by the National Council of Churches in the U.S.A., the Canadian Council of Churches, and the Secretariat for Interreligious and Ecumenical Affairs of the National Conference of Catholic Bishops. In addition, many individual communions (e.g., Presbyterian, Methodist, Lutheran, Episcopalian, United Church of Christ) have offices for interfaith work.[17] Some churches that do not participate in ecumenical structures also have established programs. The Southern Baptist Convention, the largest Protestant denomination in the United States with more than fifteen million members, has a Department for Interfaith Witness in its Home Mission Board. The program components in these institutional bodies vary, but most include educational programs and literature as well as various kinds of dialogue meetings.

These institutional programs make up only a portion of the picture. In virtually every North American city of moderate size, one can find small groups or local organizations formed to foster interreligious relations. In many settings, the primary relationships are between Christians and Jews; increasingly, adherents of other traditions are becoming active participants as well. On a recent visit to Detroit, for instance, I learned of extensive Christian-Muslim relations programs involving Arab-American groups, local mosques and churches. At that time, plans were well underway for bringing the top Muslim religious authority in Syria (the *mufti*), Shaikh Ahmad Kiftaru, to Detroit for a series of lectures and programs. The sponsor for this interfaith initiative: the Detroit Presbytery.

New interfaith coalitions and organizations are appearing each month. Some, like the U.S. Interreligious Committee for Peace in the Middle East, have a clearly established agenda. Others are concerned to explore the meaning of religious diversity as well as opportunities for cooperative efforts at the local level. Many of the new interfaith organizations include prominent leaders in the various religious communities.

Not only are interreligious organizations growing in number, they are also finding their way together. From October 30 through November 1, 1988, more than 100 representatives from different interfaith groups gathered in Wichita, Kansas, for the first North American Interfaith Conference. Participants at the gathering explored elements of spirituality in different traditions, heard and responded to speakers addressing the obstacles and opportunities facing interfaith organizations and considered topics such as the environment, peace, and justice in their respective traditions. One direct result of this conference was the strengthening of another new organization: the North American Interfaith Network.

The landscape is changing. The rapid proliferation of interfaith groups in North America is one manifestation of new institutional expressions from people whose declared motivation grows out of a life of faith. Without doubt, the quality and value of the programs initiated in the interfaith arena will vary markedly. Not all, perhaps not many, small organizations will proceed with the depth of thoughtful reflection necessary in large institutions that answer to a broad constituency. Nonetheless, it is increasingly obvious that organized efforts to stimulate, nurture, and expand interfaith relations are becoming a permanent feature in the religious landscape.

CHAPTER SIX

A Way Forward
in Christian-Muslim Relations

Christians and Muslims have traveled a long, circuitous and often bumpy road together for fourteen centuries. Nearing the end of the twentieth century, there are ominous signs that continuing mistrust and mutual antipathy combined with upheaval and rapid political change may make the journey forward even more difficult and dangerous. Recognizing the need for improving Christian-Muslim relations is not synonymous with improved relations.

Given the long history of enmity, it is clear that there are no quick fixes. There are no easy answers or simple solutions that will insure mutual understanding, respect, and cooperation between these descendants of Abraham. But the road is not blocked. There are options. There is a way forward. And there are hopeful indications that a growing number of people are recognizing and responding to the religious and socio-political impetus to work for a future wholly different from the tortured past.

Throughout this study, we have underscored the urgent need for improving interfaith relations. We have identified major impediments obstructing the path and suggested ways to deal constructively with these obstacles. Further, we have highlighted emerging opportunities for creative movement forward. We conclude this inquiry with reflections drawn from the preceding chapters, but focussed on the goal of identifying a viable way forward in Christian-Muslim relations.

EDUCATION

Education provides the basis for mutual understanding. Uninformed or erroneous views about the other, be they conscious or unconscious, are at the root of many problems plaguing Christian-Muslim relations. We need both intentional efforts to unlearn some of what we presume we know about Islam as well as to study empathetically the religious faith and traditions of Muslims. The same is generally true for Muslim understanding of the Christian tradition, though the particular dynamics differ since Muslims have a clearer starting point with the Qur'an.

The resistance to such a seemingly obvious proposition was illustrated poignantly one evening several years ago at a church where I was speaking. In the midst of questions and discussion following my presentation, one man jumped up in response to the suggestion that Christians must endeavor to understand our neighbors better if we genuinely desire to keep God's commandments not to bear false witness and to love our neighbor. Before he realized what he had said, he blurted out these words: "Don't confuse me with the facts. I already know what I believe!" More than slightly embarrassed for their friend, others found tactful ways to help him see that we all do need to be "confused by the facts."

New insights, however partial or tentative, can be unsettling. Fundamental assumptions may need to be reconsidered in light of new understandings. For some, the study of other religious traditions is particularly threatening since they fear it will lead to either syncretism or relativism. I heard this refrain from three different seminary professors prior to my departure to begin doctoral studies at Harvard. Each in his own pastoral (and slightly paternalistic) way took me for a walk or to lunch so that I might be properly advised about the dangers lurking ahead.

My experience of study and engagement with Islam, and that of most others I know, has led to a deeper understanding of, appreciation for, and commitment to the life of faith as a Christian. For some, however, deep encounter may lead to overt conversion; others try to fashion a new understanding drawing from several traditions. Dialogical encounter—intellectual and experiential—presupposes openness. Where there is openness, there is the risk—some would say the opportunity or promise—of real change.

The educational process is ongoing. We must never presuppose that we fully understand another religious tradition. For that matter, who can say with certainty that we fully understand our tradition? Anyone so bold or smug to make such a claim should pause to ponder the breadth of church history; or the history of Christian reflection on the doctrine of the atonement; or the meaning of worship for Coptic Orthodox monastics living in Egyptian desert monasteries dating from the fourth century. If the process of learning and understanding one's own tradition is openended, how much more so the study of another religious tradition.

The point here is not only that new information and new ways of understanding will require modification and refinement in our thinking. It is also imperative that we recognize how selective our information about another tradition really is. When I lecture on Islam to Christian groups, I feel keenly the limitations inherent in any outsider's attempt at such a presentation. The problem is not resolved, though it may well be better addressed, when a Muslim is doing the teaching. Even with that Muslim, no matter how well informed and broadly educated, one still sees only a portion of the picture. It makes a great deal of difference if the teacher is a Jordanian university professor or an Indonesian businessman or an Indian woman living in Germany or a militant political activist from a village in the southern Philippines. The same dynamic applies when Muslims encounter individual Christians, none of whom represent the whole tradition and each of whom speaks out of a particular historical context.

The prospect of really coming to know another tradition is daunting, but it need not immobilize us. Few people fully understand the ins and outs of economic theories and their dynamics operative in North America today. Still, most of us consider it important to learn enough about economic realities so that we can function with whatever resources are available. One does not have to be an economics professor to make decisions about buying or selling a home or investing for retirement. The operative question—in economics as well as interfaith relations—is not whether we can master a particular subject, but whether it is important enough that we will invest ourselves in the process of education.

Thoughtful study and reflection does not imply agreement. People of good will often reach very different conclusions after appropriating the same information. To commit oneself to a study process does not mean that one will necessarily alter one's views substantially. It does mean that the level of informed discussion will rise and decision-making will be less affected by unstated bias, prejudice, and misperception. In the process, the prospects for moving beyond toleration and minimal levels of civility to neighborly relations, even cooperation, are enhanced.

I have argued that the challenges present in a rapidly changing, pluralistic and interdependent world move the interfaith agenda front and center. Practical needs for mutual understanding and cooperation as well as deeper theological questions about particularity and pluralism compel us to chart a future course that is distinctively different from the past. A fundamental commitment to education, however formal or informal, is required.

In my experience, the combination of sustained academic inquiry and knowledge born of experience and personal encounter has been fruitful. The study of Islam is enhanced immeasurably when it includes personal interaction with Muslims. Joining Muslim neighbors in breaking the fast of Ramadan provides an angle of vision and a level of meaning that cannot be experienced by reading about the annual festivities. Similarly, the richness of the Jewish Passover Seder comes alive when one shares the meal and the remembrance of the Exodus with Jewish friends. These types of human interactions are one part of a larger pattern of dialogical encounter.

DIALOGICAL ENCOUNTER

We have stressed that dialogue is more than a two-way conversation. It is a stance, an orientation, an openness. Dialogue

includes a thoughtful process of listening, learning, and inter-
acting. The simple wisdom of this approach to interpersonal
relationships should be obvious; often it is not. When relationships are distorted or partially blocked by external circumstances—as is often true in Christian-Muslim relations—the
possibility for dialogical encounter is diminished. Dialogue and
mutuality in such relationships must be cultivated and nurtured.

The dialogue programs initiated by the WCC and Vatican
provide helpful indicators for Christians and Muslims who wish
to find constructive common ground for their interaction. The
experimental approaches to structured dialogue during the past
quarter century have shown the value of concentrating on particular aspects of the multidimensional relations. Whether
engaging in interpersonal conversation or an organized program,
it is useful to delineate categories and reflect on different presuppositions operative in each. Conversations focussed on theological issues are markedly different from those related to
spirituality or cooperation on social service efforts.

Sometimes well-intentioned persons, motivated by the admi-
rable desire to stimulate better relations through understanding
and cooperation, simply get a group of people together for "dialogue." The results are frequently unsatisfactory for the participants since people bring not only different perspectives, but
different expectations to the encounter. If, for instance, one
partner is anxious to discuss foundational theological issues arising in the respective scriptures and another comes with the hope
of experiencing the vitality of one another's spiritual life through
prayer and fasting, it is not likely that the two will easily connect.
Unless issues are clear and parameters are identified, the two
may talk right past one another.

The collective experience of organized dialogue can help
individuals and groups be more productive. While each dialogical encounter is unique to a particular situation, there is no
need to reinvent the wheel. Suggested guidelines, developed
through years of experience, outline some basic ground rules.

—Dialogues should be planned together whenever possible.
—Parameters for the dialogue should be considered and

identified as clearly as possible. Without being too restrictive, dialogue meetings can focus on particular concerns or issues and provide a structure (presentations, group discussion, small working groups, etc.) for addressing the issues. Ground rules can help avoid the predictable propensity many have to shift from dialogue into sermonic monologue.

— Normally, the participants should be people who speak from a perspective of faith and personal religious experience.

— Dialogue meetings should endeavor to include equal numbers of persons from each religious tradition. Further efforts to "balance" the group (for example, male/female ratios, ethnic diversity, age, etc.) should be considered in planning as they relate to the particular focus for dialogue.

— Dialogue participants should endeavor to understand the religious, cultural and ideological diversity present in the local situation, as well as the particular commitments they as individuals bring to the encounter.

— Organized efforts at a local level can benefit from an awareness of what is taking place at regional or international levels within different Christian and Muslim institutional structures. Learning from and providing input to larger processes can help facilitate interfaith relations at all levels.

These basic ground rules can assist in channeling the energies and good intentions of organizers into the most productive structural arrangements. They do not, however, limit the options for consideration in dialogue. The experimental approach implemented by the Vatican's Pontifical Council for Interreligious Dialogue in the late 1980s reminds us that many options exist — and should be explored. The ground rules suggest ways to organize the exploration.

An intriguing debate exists on the need for or value of coming into dialogue informed by a particular theological frame of reference. The Pontifical Council for Interreligious Dialogue pursues its program on the basis of an "inclusive" theological orientation. Dialogue is rooted in the recognition of truth in other religions. Partners in dialogue are approached and engaged with the assumption that they are already somehow included in the larger work of God through Christ. Some advocates for dialogue, offering variations on this approach, suggest that traditional christological understandings are too restrictive and must change prior to dialogical encounter.

Many others do not share this view. Rather, they stress that dialogue is predicated on an unreserved openness to others and an honest willingness to rethink and reformulate views. The aim is understanding, not necessarily agreement. Change may well come through learning and understanding, but dialogical encounter does not depend on such changes in advance. In fact, it may obscure the process. David Lochhead argues this position cogently in a chapter entitled, "Dialogue and Theology." He uses the example of his involvement with Christian-Buddhist encounter to clarify the point.

> In order for me to enter into dialogue with Buddhists, I do not need to change my christology any more than I expect Buddhists to become theists. Insofar as my christology is indeed a christology (and not a covert ideology of isolation or hostility), it need not be an obstacle to dialogue. All that I need to believe, for genuine dialogue to begin, is that Buddhists are not out of touch with reality. Once the fundamental sanity of Buddhists is granted, it follows that there is some point to dialogue, to understanding how the world looks through Buddhist eyes.
>
> As a Christian, I am likely to persist in my belief that Buddhists are wrong about God. I am not likely to adopt their belief that the existence or nonexistence of God is irrelevant to the spiritual quest. Nevertheless, the Buddhist critique of theism will inevitably cause me to examine and reexamine my own theistic assumptions.[1]

In addition to the serious theological and spiritual dimensions of dialogue, there are heartening practical benefits. For virtually everyone I know, dialogue meetings have provided fertile ground for nurturing close friendships. Engaging others on matters of ultimate concern for people of faith draws people together. The importance of friendships and trust across religious lines cannot be overstated. In the course of my involvements in the Iranian hostage crisis and various church-related ministries in Lebanon, Israel/Palestine, and Egypt, these friendships have been vital. Or, when the debates and demonstrations over Salman Rushdie's book were most heated, there were numerous examples where Christians and Muslims who already knew one another came together to search for constructive ways to respond and work within their respective communities. In an increasingly volatile and interdependent world, friendships and trust between Christians and Muslims—even among people who openly disagree on major issues—are signs of hope.

A good example of the personal dimension nurtured through a structured effort at interfaith cooperation is found in the U.S. Interreligious Committee for Peace in the Middle East. This organization was established in 1986 as a vehicle to bring together Jews, Christians, and Muslims who shared the concern for a negotiated settlement to the longstanding Israeli/Palestinian conflict. Among the more than 1,500 prominent religious leaders active in this organization, there are significant differences of opinion as well as views on what steps might be most productive in pursuing the elusive search for peace. While many of the differences will not be resolved, most participants have been surprised and moved by the extent to which people are in agreement on issues of self-determination, independence and security for both Israelis and Palestinians.[2]

Having worked closely with this organization, I have witnessed significant developments over five years. In addition to demonstrating that Jews, Christians, and Muslims can find agreement and work together on even the most divisive issues (such as the path toward Middle East peace), it also challenges prevailing, monolithic stereotypes about religious groups in the United States. At another level, this effort has helped foster positive, new relationships. The ease with which many religious leaders now interact personally (and, increasingly, at an institutional level) would not have been apparent only five years earlier. This informal type of dialogical encounter tends to "humanize" the other and nurture interfaith relations in ways that will extend far beyond the scope of Middle East issues.

The U.S. Interreligious Committee for Peace in the Middle East did not just happen. It developed over a period of time after careful, consultative planning. Like other, more formal interfaith encounters, it required creative leadership to channel obvious concerns into constructive engagement and productive programs.

A central thesis of this study is that intentional dialogue represents a positive way forward in the complicated and convoluted relations between Christians and Muslims. We must stress, however, that this position should not be interpreted to mean that dialogical encounter is necessarily easy or visibly positive. Genuine dialogue can be and often is intense, difficult, and even confrontational. There is no reason to assume that agreement will result when people meet and share honestly out of their deepest concerns. As is the case with other interpersonal relationships—with a spouse, siblings, one's next door neighbor— Christians and Muslims will discover points where they must simply agree to disagree.

Intentional dialogue is also comparable to family relationships and personal friendships in that both partners must work at the relationship. Mutual respect and civility may not always characterize the process of communication. The exchange can be frustrating, particularly when dialogue slips into monologue, lecturing, or preaching by one or more partners. The line of demarcation cannot always be discerned easily. Given the history of communal relations and the prejudices present among both Christians and Muslims, it is necessary to work continually at the quality of and process for the exchange.

Since interfaith dialogue relates to matters of ultimate concern for people of faith, one question that inevitably arises is that of proclamation and proselytization. Both Christianity and Islam are mission-oriented. Adherents in both communities are enjoined to proclaim the message they believe God has revealed and to encourage others to embrace the life of faith in light of God's revelation. Is proclamation and witness appropriate in the context of dialogue? In my view, the answer is no—and yes!

Dialogue should not be understood as a kind of pre-evangelization or a forum for evangelization. It is precisely the fear that Christians seek to convert Muslims that has inhibited many from dialogue, particularly in the early years when the impetus came almost exclusively from Christians. Living in the legacy of the colonial era, during which most predominantly Muslim lands were under the control of "Christian" nations of Europe, Muslims in many parts of the world remain understandably wary of dialogue as a new, more clever form of Christian mission. Some sceptics have warned others to be careful not to be lulled by some kind of "missionary trick." Few people, Christian or Muslim, will enter into dialogue with a willingness both to speak and to listen if they perceive their partners to be insincere or deceptive in representing their intentions.

Dialogue aims at mutual understanding through respectful exchange. It stands on its own, not needing justification in relation to the imperative to proclaim the central message in one's tradition. At the same time, it does not require and should not encourage people to dilute the strength of their religious commitment. Since profound exchange includes sharing what is of utmost importance, both partners must be free, even stimulated, to relate what they believe and have experienced of God's activity in human history. Far too often, people assume that an appreciation for diversity implies a lessening or playing down of one's particular religious commitment. Dialogue does not require such a stance.

Bearing witness to one's faith is perfectly appropriate in the context of dialogue. At one level, such testimony reflects the sincere commitment and rootedness of the person as a Christian or Muslim. Part of the goal of dialogue is to hear directly and learn from people whose lives are oriented around their faith and religious traditions. The distinction lies in the attitude and expectation of the participants. Dialogue is not a forum for evangelization. Participants ought not come harboring hopes or expectations of persuading others to convert. Rather, they come to speak, to listen, and to learn. A natural and authentic part of the process includes mutual witness.

Failure to clarify these distinctions will likely create confusion and frustration among dialogue participants. It may also reinforce deepseated fears and suspicions already present, particularly among people who have had negative experiences of political and/or religious domination from the other group.

A related issue complicating and inhibiting dialogue centers on power relationships. People come together in the context of various societal realities. One religious community is normally the numerical majority. Other factors—including economic, political, and social strength and influence—inevitably provide a backdrop. Persons in the minority community—Muslims in North America, Christians in Egypt, Muslims in the Philippines, Christians in Indonesia—may well feel less empowered to enter dialogue. They may be wary of their ability to speak without fear of negative consequences when "normal" relationships are resumed. Muslims and Christians with disproportionate power in their respective settings bear the major responsibility in seeking to understand and address these dynamics.

We have already indicated that the focus for dialogical encounter will vary from place to place and time to time. In many settings, the most pressing issues are also the most difficult. In a number of countries in Africa and Asia where Muslims constitute a clear majority there are political and religious leaders who advocate the implementation of the *shari'a* or Islamic law. Minority communities, including Christians, understandably fear the potential consequences of such measures no matter how careful or equitable a particular leader or political party may intend to be in preserving religious freedom and personal law. While issues related to the implementation of the *shari'a* may be paramount, they may be exceedingly difficult to approach in a given setting, particularly if Christians and Muslims have not already developed solid friendships and working relationships.

Where Christians comprise the clear majority, as is the case in Europe and North America, they must take care both to understand the most urgent agenda for Muslims and seek ways to empower the minority community to articulate its concerns. The sensitivity and desire to help insure full rights for religious minorities grows naturally out of improved relationships and friendships. It also provides an example and a frame of reference for Christians and Muslims in other settings where the issues may be more explosive.

The opportunity for dialogical encounter is present at many levels. The future for Christian-Muslim relations is inextricably linked to the understandings and relationships nurtured in various types of formal and informal exchange. Institutions and self-defined groups have substantial roles to play. But, the major burden falls on us all as individuals. Whatever outward manifestations of encounter we pursue or embrace, it is necessary to develop our awareness of and cultivate the processes for ongoing inner dialogue. We must, as people of faith, seek to make the continual task of reshaping what Diana Eck calls our "inner landscape" a self-conscious process. In so doing, we are much less likely to fall prey to smug self-righteousness and intolerance born of rigid certainty.

The deliberate move out from the intellectual safe harbor into the more uncertain deep waters of the open seas presents us with the challenges and opportunities inherent in the life of faith. It is a journey we are compelled to undertake. Who among us can claim to have exhausted the fullness of the knowledge of God's will as it speaks to our relations with God and humankind? As the Apostle Paul says, Christians must wrestle with the principalities and powers and struggle against the sins that so easily beset us. Muslims, likewise, must continually engage in *jihad*, the internal struggle with human frailties and selfish desires that make it difficult to identify and follow the will of God.

The internal struggle and inner dialogue link directly with the outward pilgrimage. In the final decade of the twentieth century and beyond into the twenty-first, this pilgrimage cannot be separated from the pilgrimage of others who share the realities and demands of an increasingly interdependent world. More than ever, the individual life of faith is bound up with the community. The inner dialogue is a critical component informing and nurturing as well as being informed and nurtured by the outward quest. Deliberate dialogical encounter—internal and external—enables Christians and Muslims to strive together in the way of God.

PRACTICAL STEPS TOWARD A NEW RELATIONSHIP

We have already suggested or implied several ways to move forward in Christian-Muslim relations. Individual and group study programs and structured dialogue meetings offer a range of options in most local settings. Prior to or in conjunction with such endeavors, concerned people can pursue other interim or complementary steps.

Christians should first find out what their own religious community (denomination, local, regional, or national council of churches) has done, is doing, or plans to do in the area of Christian-Muslim relations. Many people will be surprised to discover programs and staff working in this area in their national denominational offices. Several churches have developed policy papers or educational literature focussed on Christian-Muslim relations. Frequently, churches collaborate on interfaith issues in the context of their ecumenical structures. Thus, individual churches are often linked with regional and national programs. In cases where no program exists, people may turn to other denominational groups for assistance even as they encourage their own communion to begin work in this area.

In addition to materials produced by church-related groups, individuals may find some of the newly formed interfaith organizations to be helpful resources. For some, interfaith groups may even provide a more congenial context for educational pursuits and dialogue opportunities.

When organizing a study program, Christians should seek to include Muslims in both the planning process and the actual program. The physical presence of Muslims not only adds authenticity to the endeavor, it also provides an invaluable critique for Christians who are seeking to teach about or study Islam. Muslims ought to be able to recognize themselves and Islam in the presentations made by others. To the extent they do not, they should have opportunity to supplement a presentation. The same principle holds true when Muslims explain the Christian religious tradition to other Muslims. The only word of caution, which we have mentioned above, is that no one Christian or Muslim can speak for the entire community. The critique may be illuminating; it almost certainly will not be definitive.

The proliferation of mosques and Islamic centers throughout North America makes it possible for Christians to seek out contact with Muslim neighbors. In my experience, Muslims welcome visitors to their mosques and community centers. Institutional representatives are generally happy to provide information about Islam, the daily prayers, the meaning of religious holidays or celebrations and the like.[3]

In some settings it may be possible to arrange for reciprocal visits to one another's mosque and church. I have taken Christian groups to mosques to observe Muslims praying and then met with people who provided information and responded to questions arising from the experience. In other settings, people may prefer to begin by simply inviting Muslim speakers to address their group on a particular topic. There are many options.

Beyond educational efforts and structured dialogue, opportunities for cooperative social action abound. Obvious concerns relate to societal problems such as homelessness, poverty, and the proliferation of drugs. Not only can Christians and Muslims strengthen their common efforts by working together, they can learn from one another. Many Christian clergy and chaplains, for instance, have discovered that their Muslim colleagues have been far more successful in programs for drug and prison rehabilitation. Fighting the war against drugs and working to rehabilitate criminal offenders are proper arenas for religious communities. The success of such ministries requires the best efforts by all who share the concern. Why not learn from one another and work together?

The Qur'an speaks directly to the issue of religious diversity and the importance of constructive work in society. Human behavior is a kind of test. Assuming that people will never fully sort out the differences in their respective communities, the Qur'an challenges people to compete with one another in good works:

If God had so willed, He would have made all of you one community, but [He has not done so] that He may test you in what He has given you; so compete with one another in good works. To God you shall return and He will tell you [the truth] about that which you have been disputing. (Qur'an 5:48)

In conversation with Muslims, Christians will discover the major social and political issues facing that community. In North America and Europe, the issues frequently relate to matters the larger community takes for granted. Muslims in many settings do not enjoy the same privileges as Christians and Jews in the public recognition of their religious holidays. Dietary restrictions and dress codes often pose difficulties in public schools. There are exceptions. In the Detroit area where the Muslim population is particularly large, public schools recognize Islamic holidays and they do not serve pork in school cafeterias. After conversation with concerned parents, schools allow Muslim girls to wear slacks (rather than shorts) in gym classes and swim separately from boys.

I know of instances where the basic elements of religious freedom were set aside and Muslims were prevented from organizing for worship or building a mosque. A particular burden rests with the Christian majority to protect the rights of minority communities. Too often, Christians are unaware of the difficulties faced by North American Muslims. Or worse, Christians inspired by a vision of "Christian America," have actually led the move to deny religious freedom to the Muslim community in some settings. Such behavior not only undermines the rightly cherished principle of religious freedom, but it harms the prospects for full religious freedom for Christians living as minority communities elsewhere in the world.

Practical ways to connect, to get to know and cooperate with Muslim neighbors are all around. A simple review of issues and dominant concerns in one's own community will yield further clues in the search for areas of common concern. Morality in media and challenges posed by secularization as well as a host of community issues taken up by local churches represent natural points of contact with Muslims. Once Christians and Muslims move beyond the distorting veil of stereotypical images and numbing prejudices and approach one another as human beings who care about their families and societies, the options for better relations and cooperative ventures come more sharply into focus.

There is no simple, straightforward way to move ahead positively in Christian-Muslim relations. There are various elements which can be pursued individually or simultaneously. The intentional, collective efforts by people of good will, rooted in their community of faith, will bear fruit. The benefits will be manifest both in their societies and in the ongoing process of self-understanding in the midst of pluralism. The journey forward will surely be difficult and, undoubtedly, marked by numerous obstacles, detours, and setbacks. But, in the final decade of the 20th century, we can see more clearly than ever that we are sojourners together on that road into the future. The ways in which Christians and Muslims choose to travel that road will have profound consequences for both communities — and for the world.

Notes

1. OBSTACLES AND OPPORTUNITIES

1. See Edward W. Said, *Covering Islam: How the Media and the Experts Determine How We See the Rest of the World* (New York: Pantheon Books, 1981), for a detailed study of the media coverage of Iran in the context of a broader analysis of how the image of Islam has been and is being shaped in the West.

2. We use generic terms like "the West" and "Middle East" as convenient categories whose meanings are generally understood. Ultimately, the divisions implied by segregating the world into such geographic categories break down. Still, the terms are useful in describing, for instance, Western Christian (i.e., the majority Protestant and Roman Catholic communities in Europe and North America) perspectives on Islam in contrast to those among Middle Eastern Christians (i.e., the predominantly Orthodox communities which have lived together with Muslims for fourteen centuries).

3. In an article published in a British newspaper, *The Independent* (February 4, 1990), one year after the controversy erupted, Rushdie maintained his basic stance. Writing from an undisclosed location and under police protection, the author expressed regret that "offense had been taken against his work when none was intended." At the same time, he acknowledged that the book is, in part, "a secular man's reckoning with the religious spirit." A British immigrant from a Muslim family in Bombay, Rushdie has stated repeatedly that he has not believed in God since adolescence. Since he is not a Muslim, he has never accepted as legitimate the charge of apostasy or blasphemy.

4. See B. Haines and F. Cooley (eds.), *Christians and Muslims Together—An Exploration by Presbyterians* (Philadelphia: The Geneva Press, 1987), pp. 47-65, for a demographic, socioeconomic and sociopolitical survey of the Islamic world in 1985. This useful book features four case studies of countries (Nigeria, Indonesia, Egypt and the U.S.) where Christians and Muslims comprise different majority/minority portions of the population.

See also Ismail and Lois al-Faruqi, *The Cultural Atlas of Islam* (Macmillan: New York, 1986).

5. Some estimates put the number of Muslims in the U.S. higher than six million in 1990.

6. See Leonard Swidler, "Interreligious and Interideological Dialogue: The Matrix for all Systematic Reflection Today," pp. 7-13, in L. Swidler (ed.), *Toward a Universal Theology of Religion* (Maryknoll, N.Y.: Orbis Books, 1987), for a very helpful summary of the ways in which traditional understandings of "truth" are being reshaped through the historicization of truth, the sociology of knowledge, an appreciation of the limits of language, and the insights of hermeneutical or interpretive process.

7. Jack G. Shaheen, "The Hollywood Arab: 1984-86," *Mideast Monitor* (1986), p. 1.

8. Jack G. Shaheen, *The TV Arab* (Bowling Green, Ohio: Bowling Green State University Press, 1984).

9. Laurence Michalak, "Cruel and Unusual: Negative Images of Arabs in American Popular Culture," Issue Paper No. 15 (American Arab Anti-Discrimination Committee, 1984).

2. TOWARD UNDERSTANDING ISLAM

1. The most useful introductions to Islam include the following: Frederick M. Denny, *Islam* (San Francisco: Harper and Row, 1987), is a recent, lucid, and accessible text; Kenneth Cragg and Martin Speight, *The House of Islam* (Belmont, Calif.: Wadsworth, 3rd ed., 1988), is a compact, yet thorough volume with an accompanying anthology; R. Marston Speight, *God is One—The Way of Islam* (New York: Friendship Press, 1989), is a solid, popular introduction written primarily for Christians; H.A.R. Gibb, *Islam: A Historical Survey* (New York: Oxford University Press, 2nd rev. ed., 1970), although slightly dated, remains valuable for its brevity, scholarship, and readability; Fazlur Rahman, *Islam* (Chicago: University of Chicago Press, 2nd ed., 1979), is perhaps the best one-volume text by a prominent Muslim scholar; and Marshall G.S. Hodgson, *The Venture of Islam: Conscience and History in a World Civilization*, 3 vols. (Chicago: University of Chicago Press, 1978), is the definitive study in English.

2. Geertz, a well-known social anthropologist at Princeton, has done extensive research in the Muslim world. See Clifford Geertz, *Islam Observed: Religious Development in Morocco and Indonesia* (Chicago: University of Chicago Press, 1968), for a fascinating study of the diversity in popular piety present at two ends of the Muslim world.

3. A variety of books on the life of Muhammad are available in English. W. Montgomery Watt, *Muhammad: Prophet and Statesman* (London: Oxford University Press, 1961), remains a standard text. Martin Lings, *Muhammad: His Life Based on the Earliest Sources* (London: George Allen and Unwin, 1983), is a readable account reproducing Arabic sources.

4. See Annemarie Schimmel, *And Muhammad is His Messenger: The Veneration of the Prophet in Islamic Piety* (Chapel Hill, N.C.: University of North Carolina Press, 1985), for a thoughtful and detailed exploration of the ways Muslims have understood, celebrated, honored, and emulated the prophet.

5. W.C. Smith, *Modern Islam in India* (Lahore, India: Ashraf Press, 1943; rev. ed., 1946), p. 72.

6. Although Muslims stress that the Qur'an cannot properly be read except in Arabic, various interpretive translations exist. In English, the following texts are easily available from different publishers: *The Holy Qur'an*, translated by Yusuf Ali, includes helpful notes; *The Meaning of the Glorious Koran*, translated by Muhammad M. Pickthall, is a standard version considered accurate, but stiff in its literal renditions; *The Koran Interpreted*, translated by A.J. Arberry, is a more poetic text, capturing something of the texture in the Arabic; and *The Koran*, by J.M. Rodwell, is useful for study since it presents the text arranged in one version of the proper chronological order.

7. W.C. Smith, "Is the Qur'an the Word of God?" in *Questions of Religious Truth* (New York: Charles Scribner's Sons, 1967), pp. 49-50.

8. See Fazlur Rahman, *Major Themes of the Qur'an* (Minneapolis, Minn.: Bibliotheca Islamica, 1980), for a valuable introduction and presentation of qur'anic teachings.

9. For a short introduction see, A.J. Arberry, *Sufism: An Account of the Mystics of Islam* (London: George Allen and Unwin, 1950). A full treatment is found in Annemarie Schimmel, *Mystical Dimensions of Islam* (Chapel Hill, N.C.: University of North Carolina Press, 1975).

10. John L. Esposito, "Islamic Revivalism," *The Muslim World Today*, Occasional Paper No. 3 (Washington, D.C.: American Institute for Islamic Affairs, 1985), p. 1. Several useful studies are now available in English. John L. Esposito, *Islam: The Straight Path* (New York: Oxford University Press, 1988), provides an excellent introduction to Islam with particular emphasis on the modern period. Yvonne Y. Haddad, *Contemporary Islam and the Challenge of History* (Albany, N.Y.: State University of New York Press, 1982), offers a penetrating study of various challenges confronting Islam today. Edward Mortimer, *Faith and Power: The Politics of Islam* (New York: Random House, 1982),

presents a well-informed journalist's engaging account of political dynamics in several Muslim countries undergoing change. For two recent accounts of political activism, particularly among the Shi'ites, see Robin Wright, *Sacred Rage: The Wrath of Militant Islam* (New York: Simon and Schuster, 1985) and Robin Wright, *In the Name of God: The Khomeini Decade* (New York: Simon and Schuster, 1989).

3. THE HISTORY OF CHRISTIAN-MUSLIM RELATIONS

1. Justin Martyr, for instance, found traces of truth in pagan thinkers since he believed all the people shared in the *logos spermatikos* ("generative Word"). Clement, the renowned teacher of Origen, supplemented the divine revelation with ideas from Greek philosophy, a tradition he also considered a divine gift.

2. This is not a new discovery. In Richard Bell, *The Origin of Islam in Its Christian Environment* (London: MacMillan and Co., 1926), pp. 185-86, the Islamicist concludes: "We hear of very few cases of forced conversion to the new faith once the tide of conquest had swept over a country and passed beyond it. The Ommayad Caliphs were not conspicuous for their missionary zeal."

3. John Meyendorff, *The Orthodox Church: Its Past and Its Role in the World Today*, trans. by J. Chapin (New York: Pantheon Books, 1962), p. 83. The Muslims were very tolerant toward Christians in the early years. Daniel J. Sahas, *John of Damascus on Islam* (Leiden: E.J. Brill, 1972), p. 25, adds the following assessment: "The Syrians were not forced to convert to Islam. . . . The tolerance of the early Ummayad Caliphs was also expressed in their decision to retain the existing system in the administration as well as its official language, Greek." Moreover, the relations between the Muslims and the Byzantines in Constantinople were not totally served by the events of the seventh century. H.A.R. Gibb, *Studies on the Civilization of Islam* (Boston: Beacon Press, 1962), pp. 47-61, argues convincingly that normal trade relations continued between the Arabs and the Byzantines until 718 C.E.

4. Walter E. Kaegi, Jr., "Initial Byzantine Reactions to the Arab Conquest," *Church History*, XXXVIII (1969), pp. 139-49, surveys the references in the seventh-century Byzantine writings. He concludes that the early reactions to the conquest can best be described as the "non-Chalcedonian" Christian attempts to offer facile explanations of the conquest as irrefutable examples of divine retribution for Calcedonian errors of the Byzantine government and the sins of the Christian church in general.

5. See Sahas, *John of Damascus on Islam*, for a thorough study of

John's engagement with the early Muslim community.

6. R.W. Southern, *Western Views of Islam in the Middle Ages* (Cambridge, Mass.: Harvard University Press, 1962), pp. 5-6.

7. Norman Daniel, *Islam and the West: The Making of an Image* (Edinburgh: Edinburgh University Press, 1960).

8. Dante Alighieri, *The Divine Comedy*, trans. by Lawrence G. White (New York: Pantheon Books, 1948), Canto 28, Line 35, p. 49.

9. A study of the Cluniac corpus is found in James Kritzeck, *Peter the Venerable and Islam* (Princeton, N.J.: Princeton University Press, 1964).

10. Thomas Michel, "Christianity and Islam: Reflections on Recent Teachings of the Church," *Encounter*, No. 112 (February, 1985), p. 3. Michel also notes that St. Francis' *Canticle for All Creatures* praises God in phrases reminiscent of the Qur'an.

11. Southern, *Western Views of Islam in the Middle Ages*, pp. 67–109. Norman Daniel, *The Arabs and Mediaeval Europe* (London: Longman Group Ltd., 1975), p. 307, agrees that "a glimmering light of understanding persisted . . . in the fifteenth century."

12. See James Biechler, *The Religious Language of Nicholas of Cusa*, Dissertation Series, No. 8 (Missoula, Mont.: Scholars Press, 1975).

13. George E. Forell, "Luther and the War against the Turks," *Church History*, XIV (1945), pp. 269-70.

14. Martin Luther, *On War Against the Turks*, trans. by C.M. Jacobs and R.C. Schultz in *Luther's Works*, ed. by H.T. Lehmann (Philadelphia: Fortress Press, 1967), pp. 170-77.

15. The Sabaeans remain a mysterious community. Some scholars feel the name may refer to the Mandaeans of southern Iraq.

16. Muzammil Siddiqi documents this point in the first chapter of his unpublished Harvard Ph.D. dissertation, "Muslim Views of Christianity in the Middle Ages: An Analytical Study of Ibn Taymiyah's Work on Christianity." See also Jacques Waardenburg, "World Religions as Seen in the Light of Islam," in *Islam: Past Influence and Present Challenge*, ed. by A. Welch and P. Cachia (Edinburgh: Edinburgh University Press, 1979), pp. 245-75.

17. See Eric J. Sharpe, *Comparative Religion: A History* (New York: Charles Scribner's Sons, 1975), for a detailed study of the history of the discipline.

18. Wilfred Cantwell Smith, "Comparative Religion: Whither — and Why?" in *The History of Religions: Essays in Methodology*, ed. by M. Eliade and J.M. Kitagawa (Chicago: University of Chicago Press, 1959), p. 34.

19. Ibid., p. 47.

20. Fredrich Heiler, "The History of Religions as a Preparation for the Co-operation of Religions," in *The History of Religions: Essays in Methodology*, ed. by M. Eliade and J.M. Kitagawa (Chicago: University of Chicago Press, 1959), pp. 137-39, 160.

21. Hendrik Kraemer, *The Christian Message in a Non-Christian World* (London: Edinburgh House Press, 1938), p. 36.

22. William E. Hocking, *Re-Thinking Missions: A Laymen's Inquiry After One Hundred Years* (New York: Harper and Brothers, 1932), p. 327.

23. Kraemer, *The Christian Message in a Non-Christian World*, pp. 122 and 302.

24. E. Stanley Jones, "Where Madras Missed its Way," in *The Guardian* (Madras), February 23, 1939, p. 102.

25. "Report on the Word of God and the Living Faiths of Men," (manuscript in the archives of the World Council of Churches, Geneva), July, 1958.

26. Kenneth Cragg, *The Call of the Minaret* (London: Oxford University Press, 1956; 2nd rev. edition, Maryknoll, N.Y.: Orbis Books, 1985).

4. CHRISTIAN PARTICULARITY AND RELIGIOUS PLURALISM

1. Harvey Cox uses this passage in the title of his provocative exploration on his encounter with other traditions of faith. See Harvey Cox, *Many Mansions* (Boston: Beacon Press, 1988).

2. Wesley Ariarajah, *The Bible and People of Other Faiths* (Geneva: World Council of Churches, 1985; U.S. edition, Maryknoll, N.Y.: Orbis Books, 1989), p. 22.

3. Ibid., p. 23.

4. There are any number of books and articles one might consult for further exploration. See, for instance, Chapter IX, "How is Jesus Unique? Toward a Theocentric Christology" in Paul Knitter, *No Other Name? A Critical Survey of Christian Attitudes Toward the World Religions* (Maryknoll, N.Y.: Orbis Books, 1985), pp. 171–204.

5. Ibid., pp. 25–6.

6. See footnote 6 in chapter 1.

7. Kenneth Cracknell, *Towards a New Relationship: Christians and People of Other Faith* (London: Epworth Press, 1986), pp. 69–70.

8. Ibid., pp. 79–86.

9. Ibid., pp. 103, 106–7.

10. Ibid., p. 108.

11. John B. Cobb, *Beyond Dialogue: Toward a Mutual Transformation*

of Christianity and Buddhism (Philadelphia: Fortress Press, 1982), p. vii.

12. See, for instance, the following: Knitter, *No Other Name? A Critical Survey of Christian Attitudes Toward the World Religions*; Alan Race, *Christians and Religious Pluralism: Patterns in the Christian Theology of Religions* (Maryknoll, N.Y.: Orbis Books, 1982); and Gavin D'Costa, *Theology and Religious Pluralism* (London: Basil Blackwell Ltd., 1986).

13. Race, *Christians and Religious Pluralism*, p. 38. See Knitter, *No Other Name?*, pp. 120–44, and D'Costa, *Theology and Religious Pluralism*, pp. 80–116, for detailed analyses of inclusivist theologies.

14. Austin P. Flannery, ed., *Documents of Vatican II*, 2nd ed. (Grand Rapids, Mich.: Wm. B. Eerdmans, 1980), p. 738.

15. Ibid., p. 739.

16. Ibid., pp. 739–40.

17. Ibid., pp. 740–42.

18. Ibid., p. 367.

19. Karl Rahner, *Theological Investigations*, Vol. 5 (Baltimore, Md.: Helicon, 1966), pp. 118, 121, 131, and 133.

20. Some theologians reverse this and speak of Christianity as the extraordinary path among a host of ordinary or normal ways present in the world.

21. See "Pope's Christmas Address to the Roman Curia," *Bulletin — Secretariatus pro non Christianis*, XXII, No. 1 (1987), pp. 54–62.

22. Knitter, *No Other Name?*, p. 147. For their respective treatments of pluralist positions, see Knitter, pp. 145–67; D'Costa, *Theology and Religious Pluralism*, pp. 22–51; and Race, *Christians and Religious Pluralism*, pp. 70–105.

23. John Hick, *God and the Universe of Faiths* (New York: St. Martin's Press, 1973), p. 131.

24. John Hick, *God Has Many Names* (London: MacMillan, 1980), p. 6.

25. See W.C. Smith, *Towards a World Theology: Faith and the Comparative History of Religion* (Philadelphia: Westminster Press, 1981; Maryknoll, N.Y.: Orbis Books, 1990) and *The Meaning and End of Religion* (New York: New American Library, 1963).

26. John Hick and Paul F. Knitter (eds.), *The Myth of Christian Uniqueness: Toward a Pluralistic Theology of Religions* (Maryknoll, N.Y.: Orbis Books, 1987), p. vii.

27. See Gavin D'Costa (ed.), *Christian Uniqueness Reconsidered: The Myth of a Pluralistic Theology of Religions* (Maryknoll, N.Y.: Orbis Books, 1990). In a recent address given at Georgetown University, an Indian Jesuit, Fr. Michael Amaladoss, set forth a provocative fourth

paradigm: pluralism in unity. The following two paragraphs provide a glimpse into his perspective and, at the same time, illustrate the range of serious theological reflection among Christians worldwide.

"At the phenomenological, historical level, a real pluralism and diversity of religions is acknowledged. But immanent to this pluralism is a dynamic structure of unity. This principle of unity is the one plan of God for the world. Unity is therefore the horizon that does not destroy, but includes and transcends the diversity. But this unity is not given, but is to be achieved in and through the historical process. The Scriptural symbol for this unity is the reign of God. All the peoples are called to it and are moving toward it (Eph 1:9–10; Col 1:15–20; 1 Cor 15:28; Rev 21:1–5). God's own self-communication in the world through the Word and the Spirit, in various ways and at various times, is ordained to this (Jn 1:3, 9; Heb 1:1-2). The Spirit is really the active principle of this process (Rom 8). It is in the context of this global dynamism that the church is called to discover its own identity. The church does not identify itself with the reign of God. It is, however, aware of being its symbol and servant. It considers this its special vocation. This is its mission: to serve the realization of the reign of God in the world.

"Unity is not the only attribute of this reign. In other contexts one could talk of liberation, of humanization, of development, of fulfillment, of reconciliation, etc. The church does not proclaim itself, but the reign. Once the church becomes aware of the role of other religions in the plan of God, the church does not simply identify its own growth with the growth of the reign. The other religions, too, have their roles to play in this history, which is at the same time a cosmic mystery. The realization of the reign need not be seen as the whole world becoming church, but as the unification and reconciliation of all things and peoples, with all their gifts and creations, in Christ and in the Spirit."

See, Fr. Michael Amaladoss, S.J., "Rationales for Dialogue with World Relgions," *Origins* (January, 1990), pp. 572–77.

28. See Hans Küng, et al., *Christianity and the World Religions: Paths to Dialogue with Islam, Hinduism and Buddhism* (New York: Doubleday, 1986), pp. 19–36, 50–69, 83–96 and 109–130.

29. Ibid., pp. 25–6.

30. Ibid., pp. 27–8. The problem for Christian theology turns, in part, on whether the prophetic experience of Muhammad is understood as private or public. If the revelation is viewed as public, the role of Muhammad's prophethood must be explained in relation to the role of the Bible.

31. Ibid., p. 27.

32. See W.C. Smith, "Is the Qur'an the Word of God", pp. 39–62.

33. Küng, *Christianity and World Religions*, pp. 28–33.

5. THE DIALOGUE MOVEMENT

1. David Lochhead, *The Dialogical Imperative: A Christian Reflection on Interfaith Encounter* (Maryknoll, N.Y.: Orbis Books, 1988), p. 80.

2. Ibid., p. 81.

3. Diana L. Eck, "What Do We Mean by 'Dialogue'?" *Current Dialogue*, No. 11 (December, 1986), pp. 5–15.

4. Knitter, *No Other Name?*, p. 206. John Borelli makes a similar case for the importance of the history of religions. He argues persuasively that the study of "other traditions" is vital for Christians at many levels, not the least of which relates to self-understanding. See John Borelli, "Religious Studies: Context for Ecumenism," *Ecumenical Trends* (December, 1984), pp. 104–6.

5. Eck, "What Do We Mean by 'Dialogue'?", p. 11.

6. Thomas Merton, "Monastic Experience and East-West Dialogue," (Notes for a paper to have been delivered at Calcutta, October 1968) in *Bulletin — Secretariatus Pro Non-Christianis*, XXVII (1988), pp. 21-2.

7. Eck, "What Do We Mean by 'Dialogue'?", pp. 14–15.

8. For the full text of the Broumana memorandum (and other early WCC documents), see *Christians Meeting Muslims — WCC Papers on Ten Years of Christian-Muslim Dialogue* (Geneva: World Council of Churches, 1977), pp. 89–96.

9. Among the numerous DFI publications are the following: *Courage for Dialogue, Christians and Education in a Multi-Faith World, The Bible and People of Other Faiths, Ministerial Formation in a Multifaith Milieu,* and *Meeting in Faith: Twenty Years of Christian-Muslim Conversations Sponsored by the WCC*. A complete list of publications in print is available from the WCC offices in New York or Geneva.

10. Diana L. Eck, "On Seeking and Finding in the World's Religions," *The Christian Century* (May 2, 1990), p. 455.

11. Pope Paul VI, *Ecclesiam Suam* (Vatican City: Tipographia Poliglotta Vaticana, 1964), pp. 69–70.

12. The most comprehensive study of the Vatican Secretariat for Non-Christians is found in Robert B. Sheard, *Interreligious Dialogue in the Catholic Church Since Vatican II: An Historical and Theological Study* (Lewiston, N.Y.: Edwin Mellen Press, 1987). For a shorter, but very helpful treatment of the historical development of officially sanctioned Catholic interfaith programs and documents, see John F. Hotchkin and

John Borelli, "Roman Catholic Interreligious Offices and Documents," in *The Handbook for Interreligious Dialogue*, ed. by John Borelli (Morristown, N.J.: Silver, Burdett and Ginn, 1990), pp. 51–6.

13. M. de Gigord and J. Pereira, "Asian Bishops Meet at Kuala Lumpur (13-20 November, 1979), *Encounter—Documents for Muslim-Christian Understanding*, IV, No. 66 (June-July, 1980), p. 11.

14. "The Attitude of the Church Toward the Followers of Other Religions (Reflections and Orientations on Dialogue and Mission)," (Vatican City: Secretariatus Pro Non Christianis, 1984), pp. 10–11.

15. Ibid., pp. 14–15.

16. See Thomas Michel, "Pope John Paul II's Teaching about Islam in his Addresses to Muslims," *Bulletin: Secretariatus pro non Christianis*, XXI, No. 2 (1986), pp. 182–91, and regular updates in the *Bulletin* for documentation on the wide-ranging concerns in the discourses of the pontiff.

17. A few denominational bodies have commissioned or supported the development of educational literature. In addition to B. Haines and F. Cooley (eds.), *Christians and Muslims Together—An Exploration by Presbyterians* noted in Chapter One above see Frank W. Kios, C. Lynn Nakumura and Daniel F. Martensen (eds.), *Lutherans and the Challenge of Religious Pluralism* (Minneapolis, Minn.: Augsburg Press, 1990).

6. A WAY FORWARD

1. Lochhead, *The Dialogical Imperative*, p. 93.

2. *The Los Angeles Times* and many U.S. papers using the *LA Times* wire service featured an editorial article co-authored by four members of the Board of Directors for the U.S. Interreligious Committee for Peace in the Middle East. See, Rabbi Arthur Hertzberg, Father Theodore Hesburgh, Rev. Charles Kimball, and Mr. Cherif Sedki, "The Faiths Must Unite to Press a Vision of Peace," *The Los Angeles Times* (June 18, 1990), p. B5.

3. Yvonne Haddad has studied and written extensively on Islam in America. Her writings provide invaluable information on the development of Muslim communities and prominent issues they face in North America. See Yvonne Y. Haddad and Adair T. Lummis, *Islamic Values in the United States* (New York: Oxford University Press, 1987) and Yvonne Y. Haddad, "A Century of Islam in America," Occasional Paper No. 4 in *The Muslim World Today* (Washington, D.C.: The Middle East Institute, 1986).